Between Fires

a memoir

Marilee Zdenek

*For Peggy & Rich,
Wishing you the best
of all you can imagine
Marlee
Zdenek*

TwoRoads
PUBLISHING

Books by Marilee Zdenek

The Right-Brain Experience
Inventing the Future
Splinters in My Pride
Someone Special
God is a Verb!
Catch the New Wind

(*God is a Verb!* and *Catch the New Wind*
were written in collaboration with Marge Champion.)

Between Fires

Copyright © Marilee Zdenek 2014
Print Edition published by Two Roads Publishing,
a division of Right-Brain Resources, Inc.
established in 1983, Santa Barbara, California

Cover design by Tammy Seidick
Cover Image © Jon Wimberely
Portrait of the author by photographer, Shannon Jayne.
Digital formatting by A Thirsty Mind Book Design

ISBN: 978-0692228098

My Life in the Palm of His Hand
copyright © 2008 Cameron Somers

Passages adapted from:

Splinters in my Pride, copyright © 1979 Marilee Zdenek
The Right Brain Experience, copyright © 1983 Marilee Zdenek
Someone Special, copyright © 1977 Marilee Zdenek

Additional Library of Congress Cataloging-in-Publication Data
available upon request.
1. Memoir 2. Hollywood 3. Santa Barbara, California 4. Paris, France
5. Grief 6. Loss 7. Spiritual 8. Inspirational
9. Right Brain studies 10. Healing

With Gratitude

For my two husbands,
Leonard S. Picker and Albert N. Zdenek MD.
who, sequentially, gave me years of happiness
and memories to last a lifetime.
I will always love them both.

Contents

The Gathering of Stories

The sharing of stories has been around since cavewomen circled the fire on cold winter nights. Together they figured out how to move on when times were hard, to feel less lonely in the search for meaning in their lives. Elders told of dangers and victories and dreams. The stories of one strengthened another. Later, women shared as they washed clothes in the rivers, then as they sewed quilts in log cabins, and later still, as they drank lattes in coffee shops and malls.

In this memoir, I want to add my story to the ones that came before. As wonderful as my life used to be, it's different now; the future will have to be wonderful in a different way. The species that doesn't adapt, doesn't survive and that's true of widows, too.

I learned that when I was twenty-seven. My husband died eighteen days after a fire burned our home to the ground. My first-born was three years old and my baby not yet one. Grief takes its time to heal, but when you have babies, you don't have that time. You just hold them and love them and do what needs to be done the best way you can. When you're in your twenties and the man you love suddenly dies, you ask yourself two obvious questions: "Who am I without him? And then: "What do I do now?"

The same questions are relevant now that I'm on the shady side of seventy and again write the words, 'My husband died.' This time I live alone and there are no more babies to distract me from grief. This time my options are different. But the emotions are the same.

What is the value of reliving the times I laughed the

hardest, danced the wildest, risked everything for love? How does it help to realize that the lessons learned through dangerous choices and wise ones, lucky ones and embarrassing ones—were all a preparation for the important ones I must make in this season of my life?

Willa Cather said, "There are only two or three human stories and they keep repeating themselves over and over again..."

It's the details that differ. The emotions are universal.

When you have loved and lost two extraordinary men, survived the grief and the challenges, you've probably gained some valuable insights about the process of healing.

Winston Churchill said, "The farther backward you can look, the farther forward you are likely to see." He was talking about world history, but it's just as applicable to my life...and perhaps to yours. I'm in the process of re-inventing my life. Before you read this, I will have turned eighty. This is a very good year. The wrenching aspects of loss have settled into a quiet gratitude for all that was, and is, and all that will be.

This is my story. This is who I am at eighty. These memories are the hands that shape the woman I will become in this next decade. And maybe the one after that.

Marilee Zdenek

Wildfires

The fire started on the north slope of the Santa Monica Mountains, miles from our home. Santa Anna winds rolled in from the desert, tumbling hard across the canyons on that hot November morning. At 8:15, a spark ignited the parched brush that quickly turned to flame as the winds caught it, then tossed it wildly from shrub to grass to limbs of trees. The fire was far away. I couldn't even smell the smoke.

Winds blew harder; the fire rose, then soared, then rode on its own heat across the thirsty hillsides of Bel Air. I didn't see the flames arch over the summit to leap across Mulholland Drive. In the distance, sirens wailed and I looked outside where dark smoke blew high and wild, still so far away. I didn't know our lives were in danger.

I would have told you, if you had asked, that I was the luckiest woman in the world. My husband was loving and loved, our two baby girls, healthy, beautiful and adored. We lived in a house my father built on Stradella Road, on the Los Angeles side of the mountain. It was a small but lovely home with a view of mountains and city lights. Sometimes, around dawn, an occasional deer showed up on our lawn. My life seemed as close to perfect as the world could offer.

On that hot November morning, miles away, the winds grew meaner. The fire fed on eucalyptus, birch and oak; houses burned, walls of glass collapsed on beds and chairs, tables and toys. It sucked life from deer and bobcats, swept across the lairs of coyotes, raging through the nests of doves.

I checked the news on TV, watching firemen hose the flames in Malibu. There was no mention of a fire in Bel Air.

Even so, I left the television on, and switched channels from time to time. I didn't know another fire was burning in the East.

My husband was at his office. My mother was visiting us, rocking my baby in the chair where she once rocked me. Eleven month-old Tamara slept peacefully, delicate as a porcelain doll. I read to Gina, my dark-eyed beauty, only three years old with two dimples in cherub cheeks. Our dog, Sassy, slept beside her.

I walked out the front door, just checking. Black smoke rose above the hills of Malibu, heavier than before. Ashes rode in the gusts of wind and now you could smell the destruction. I ached for the people whose homes were burning. And for those who might be hurt—or worse, and for all the wild creatures that were terrified, not knowing which way to turn.

Gina was anxious so I went inside to read to her again, keeping an eye on televised images of the fire's advancing line. It seemed as though all of Malibu was burning.

Sassy sensed our tension and started whining so I followed her across the room to a sliding door that opened into our back yard. I pushed the drapes aside and saw a high wall of flames billowing up the canyon toward our house. I screamed and my mother came running with the baby. When she saw the fire she yelled, "Get in the car!" and grabbed her keys from the mantle as she ran toward the door. I held Gina and we fled toward the street, slipping her through the open window of the back seat of the car. Both girls were crying but my mother's voice was firm and confident. I don't remember the words, just the tone, as she fastened my baby in her car seat. In all of my life, I never saw my mother panic.

"I have to get Sassy!" My words tumbled in the wind as I ran back to the house. "Get a hotel and call Leonard. Tell him where you are. I'll call his office when I get down the hill. Hurry!" Sassy ran frantically back and forth barking at the flames until I grabbed her and forced her into my car. Was there time to get *anything* from the house? I ran back inside, hoping to salvage something but could only risk grabbing photographs of my children and Tamara's baby blanket that lay crumpled on the floor. I saw the flames racing toward me, enveloping the trees, greedy for more. I fled in panic. *Where were my car keys!* Seconds were wasted before I remembered I had left them in my car.

Traffic was slow on the narrow road that wound down the mountain toward Sunset Boulevard. What if there was an accident? Or a car stalled, backing out of the driveway? If this road was blocked, there was no other way down the hill.

Sassy was terrified, whining and yapping, trying to get in my lap, scratching on the window, jumping to the floor. I pushed her away, holding her back with one hand. Finally, I made it to Sunset Boulevard where we were safe but there were no public phones. I kept driving and finally saw one near a gas station. But when I called, Leonard wasn't there. His secretary said he left for home as soon as he heard about the fire. *Where was he!* There was a message from my mother, leaving me the name of the motel where she waited with the girls. I drove as fast as I could. Then, when I saw them, I scooped my babies in my arms, rocking them back and forth, grateful for their safety.

It was my ever-practical mother who arranged for food and diapers, kibble for the dog, toothpaste and brushes.

Time passed and still I hadn't heard from my husband. The imagination can create such excruciating scenarios in times of crises. And when you're scared, it's hard to deceive children, but I tried. Unsuccessfully. Even our dog knew something was not right.

I heard a car pulling to a stop outside our room and flung open the door. Leonard was getting out of his car and I ran into his arms. He looked exhausted, but his smile was tender and his deep voice was rich with gratitude. I was concerned about his sudden, rasping cough but he explained—"They had the road blocked so I left the car and ran up the hill before they could stop me. The smoke was so thick I could barely see the house. Thank God I saw that the carport was empty—I was afraid you might still be there!" His story unfolded as we went into the room, Gina in his arms, Tamara in mine.

There was a long gash in his shirt. "What happened?" I asked.

"Some guy down the road was trying to save his house, which of course he couldn't do. I had to convince him to leave and he fought me off. At first, anyway. He just panicked but he's okay now."

"I want us to go first thing in the morning and see what we have left."

I saw him hesitate, glance toward the anxious faces of Gina and Tamara, and change the subject.

When the girls finally fell asleep, we carried them into the adjoining room, where my mother was settling down for the night. I will never forget the sweetness of watching my children curled safely with their grandmother in her bed, small chairs pushed against one side so the little one couldn't roll off. Like kittens, they were, snuggling close in safe arms.

"About the house..." I said, as I closed the door between rooms.

His voice was tender but his words were wrenching. "There is no house, darling."

"Everything couldn't have burned!"

"The house exploded, Marilee. I saw it happen. It literally exploded from the heat of the flames. There's nothing left." He waited while I took that in.

I heard the words but resisted the truth of them. I was sure *something* would be there.

We watched the story unfold on TV: the devastation, the chaos, and the grief-stricken faces of those who told of their losses, until I couldn't watch anymore.

It was November 6, 1961, the date of the most disastrous fire in Southern California's history. It raged on into the night, and the night after that, the black sky turning mauve above flames that rose to lick at stars.

Later, I heard that even if firemen had come to Stradella Road, there would have been no water in the hydrants. People in the flatlands of Westwood were watering their roofs, just in case.

The fire was contained at 4:00 in the morning on the third day. Later that morning, the streets were open again so we drove slowly up Stradella Road. It looked like a war zone. Nothing stood. Nothing but chimneys, stone markers where houses died. Everything there, buried in ashes. Then we saw the place where our home had been. The only thing remaining was the charred skeleton of a swing set, and the stone chimney that rose above the rubble.

I counted the losses, re-lived the history of things—my mother's, my grandmother's, my great-grandmother's collections—now gone.

Four hundred and eighty-four homes burned in that fire. Even before the ashes cooled, we were just one of those hundreds of families trying to figure out what to do.

Later, friends came to help us dig through the crusted ashes. There was only one thing I asked for in my prayer; it was something my father gave me when I was a little girl. On a bracelet, there was a gold charm that was the shape of a football with a tiny diamond in the center. It belonged to my father when he was young and played quarterback for his school. He died on December 7, 1959; that was almost two years before the fire, and now I had nothing tangible that was his, nothing he had touched.

We never found the exquisite rose quartz carving that was from my husband's father, nor could we separate my grandmother's silver that had fused to pipes in the kitchen. But in the living room, lying among the rubble, two unbroken Dresden demitasse cups survived. They exploded from the kitchen and flew over the dining room to the far side of the living room, landing remarkably intact, though I can't imagine how. There wasn't even a chip on the delicate edging, although the colors were completely burned off.

"Marilee, look!" Leonard said, "Open your hands," and in them he dropped the bracelet with the gold football attached. "I found it under a mound of ashes where your dresser used to be." There it was, along with my great-grandmother's tiny wedding band, and a collection of charms Leonard bought for me, reminders of special events in our lives.

"This is all we have." I clutched the bracelet in gratitude and disbelief.

"We may not have *things*, but we have our family and that's all we need." I remember how Leonard looked at me; how calm he was, as if he were free from the weight of possessions. My perspective was far less evolved.

That night, as we lay in our bed at the motel on Wilshire Boulevard, the shock was settling in and I tried to face the reality of our situation. Leonard wasn't interested in making plans. "Take some time for gratitude. More than four hundred houses burned and it's a miracle that no one died. And just look at our beautiful, healthy girls! Everything will work out just fine. It's just *things* that burned."

They say that men fall in love through their eyes and women through their ears and there's probably some truth in that. I know it was the soft, deep timbre of Leonard's voice that won my heart years ago, before my mind even considered the risk I was taking as I gradually fell in love with this complicated man. But before I knew about complicated, I knew about charisma and emotional honesty and wit and integrity. It's also true that he was tall with broad shoulders and dark expressive eyes that could melt an ice sculpture from a distance. Playful dimples nipped into his olive-toned cheeks so I'll admit that my eyes were involved in this process of adoration. Was he handsome? Not in the Hollywood sense of the word. Was he charming? Oh, yes.

I remember his laugh and how much I enjoyed the sound of it. He was an attorney who was spiritual, a man who loved opera, literature and philosophy. He read books I never would have chosen and taught me to love them too. On Saturday mornings, when Gina was a tiny baby, he would hold her in his lap and listen to Leonard Bernstein conducting the New York Philharmonic. Then Tamara was born and she was soon part of the ritual. He took so much pleasure in his girls.

I worked hard to accept the losses and to focus on the fact that my family was safe, and that in all of the dozens of fires that ravaged the city in those days and nights, not one life was lost.

Disasters seem to bring out the best in people. Outstretched arms were everywhere. Leonard and I, with Gina, Tamara, my mother and our dog, stayed for a couple of weeks with a family whose home had survived the flames. Then, people we barely knew loaned us a small house that was up for sale in Van Nuys. We could stay there until we decided what to do, where to go. Two weeks after the fire, we moved in. My mother was staying in an apartment near by.

I thought the worst was over. I was wrong.

Eighteen days after the fire, I lay down beside Leonard in the borrowed bed and fell asleep in rhythm with his breath. Sometime in the night, I woke to terrifying sounds that shook me to my core. I heard fierce animal noises that seemed to come from a nightmare. "Leonard, wake up, you're dreaming!" He wasn't dreaming though. I shook him, pleaded with him to wake up but there was no response, just the rasping guttural sounds that I did not understand. Something was terribly wrong with my husband. I didn't know what to do. There was no phone in the bedroom. I couldn't bear to leave him but I had to get help. I was disoriented. It wasn't my house. *Where was the phone!* I ran to the kitchen, remembering a yellow phone hanging on the wall. I called for help but couldn't remember where I was— *what was the address of this house!* Then I saw it written on a flyer lying on the counter. As soon as I hung up the phone, I ran back to Leonard. The sounds were different now but just as frightening. He stared toward the wall, unresponsive, unseeing.

Then I heard Gina beside me and she was crying. I didn't want her to see him like this but she refused to leave him. I picked her up and ran past the room where Tamara lay sleeping in her crib, then out the door to try to find a neighbor to help. *Someone might know what to do!* It was dark and I ran with Gina in my arms. I stumbled on a sprinkler head but ignored the pain of metal tearing skin and my daughter's frantic wailing as we cut through the bushes to the house next door. I slammed my hand on the doorbell and kept screaming, *"Help me! Please!"* but no one came. I tried the next house, banging on the door and crying but no lights turned on. No one answered. I ran back to the house to be with Leonard.

I put my lips on his and tried to breathe my life into his. A man appeared from nowhere but I had no idea who he was. He pounded on Leonard's chest, counting breaths, telling me to breathe into my husband's mouth. Breathe! He yelled.

The sounds stopped. The man stepped back. I put my head on Leonard's chest but I heard only silence. My husband died before dawn on Thanksgiving morning.

The house filled with people. Someone brought my mother. Someone made phone calls. Someone made coffee. In a room full of people, I was alone, without Leonard.

I didn't know the neighbors. But a few of them came to

try and help. With tears in her eyes, a woman said she heard me calling but was afraid to open the door; another thought she was dreaming. Another neighbor was a doctor, but his house was to the right; I had turned left. Fog begins to roll over the memories. I just know that there was not enough air to breathe. For days, I couldn't bear the taste of food.

If it had not been for a strong spiritual grounding, the comfort of people I loved, and two baby girls who needed their momma, I don't know how I would have gotten through this. Sometimes, I felt that invisible arms were supporting me and keeping me from falling. A doctor told me Leonard's heart attack wasn't related to the fire. I don't believe that.

No matter what your situation is, security is an illusion. One moment you think you're safe. Then you're not.

Leonard's death was the defining moment of my life. Like widows before me and after me, I did the best I could to comfort my children. How do you explain this loss to a three year old who was so close to her father? How do you comfort a baby who just wants to be held and clutches her blanket as if that's all that holds her to the planet? My biggest mistake was never to let them see me cry. My tears would have shown them that I was grieving too, but I didn't have that insight at the time.

I tried to say the right words but they were inevitably the wrong ones and they failed to comfort. I held Gina close and told her that her daddy was in Heaven, that he loved her very much. I told her God had a reason and someday we would understand. She pointed her finger to the ceiling and a cold little voice said, "God was wrong!"

I didn't tell her I thought so too.

While grieving for the man I loved, I faced other harsh realities: I had no home and no possessions; I was no longer an actress, no longer the wife of a motion picture executive. I had no confidence in how to proceed with my life, let alone raise two little girls on my own. I had never earned a consistent income. When Leonard's brother, Eugene, asked me if we had any securities, I didn't even know what that meant.

The fact remains that I come from tough pioneer stock. The stiff-upper-lip kind that does what must be done. The list of do's and don'ts was extensive in my childhood home; courage was expected and to complain was almost as serious an offense to the family code as telling a lie—which they considered tantamount to treason. The only falsehood permitted was to lie about the depth of one's feelings. And I knew how to do that well. Words from my childhood guided me now. "Whatever happens in your life, you will be given the strength to deal with it."

No matter that your heart was shattered, your body aching from the implosion of grief, you made coffee for those who stopped by, you chose a coffin, you played on the floor with your children, you signed papers without reading them, you stared into the past in the loneliness of night and prayed for the support of Spirit. And when morning came, you willed strength to come. Friends arrived, and then you comforted those who came to comfort you.

I couldn't bear to stay in the house where Leonard died, where there were no comforting memories to console me. Only days after the funeral, I told my mother, "I want to build again. I want to build the house back just like it was. Will you draw the plans for me?"

Gently she told me, "You can't do that. You have to honor Leonard's promise." Days before my husband died, a builder made an offer to buy the land. Leonard accepted and they shook hands on the deal.

"Yes I know—but he didn't know that he would die!"

"They agreed to the conditions of sale, Marilee. They were drawing the papers. You can't build there." Her eyes were stern when she said, "Leonard gave his word."

Still I pleaded, "But I could talk with that man, tell him how much I need my home." I was sixteen when my father built the house that my mother designed, the house Leonard bought from her after my father's death. "I want to build it back exactly as it was! Please, you need to support me in this!"

"You need to honor your husband's commitment. Even if you could build the house exactly as it was, it wouldn't bring Leonard back. *That's* what you really want. You want your husband back and you want your life back but it doesn't work that way. That part of your life is over. You have to accept it and move on."

I did not want to hear that. I was twenty-seven years old.

Against the Odds

In the days and weeks after Leonard's passing, friends said how strong I was and there were times when that was true. Whether it was the psychological shock that deferred the pain, or my spiritual faith or the compassion of my spiritual community or my love for our two babies that got me through those first long days and nights, I don't know. I know I did what had to be done. And nothing was as healing as holding those two little ones in my arms. It was months later, about the time everyone thought I should be moving on with my life, that I was hit by the depth of grief and the harsh reality of my situation. Moving on? I was just trying to stay afloat in the present. If you're lost in a storm at sea and the waves are smashing over your small boat, you're not thinking about long range planning.

I can't say it was love at first sight when Leonard and I first met, quite by accident, at Goldwyn Studios. My agent had brought me there that morning to meet a certain director and wanted him to cast me for a small role in his upcoming production. I had played in numerous stage shows, a few TV shows, and studied with Estelle Harman who was a fine acting coach, but I had no reputation at all. I was surprised when my agent brought another girl with us to the meeting. And I was devastated when he started raving about her and saying how perfect she would be for the part. He didn't even show my portfolio or discuss my background. Other than acknowledging the introduction, I don't think the director said a word to me. What a scumbag my agent was! Why did he bring me there? What was going on? I'll never know. I do know that I felt humiliated and angry. I had been so excited about the opportunity but this was no opportunity at all. I couldn't wait to get off the Goldwyn lot.

When the meeting was over, I didn't say a word to my agent because I was so angry I wouldn't risk what I might say. I was twenty years old, from a "proper" family and not experienced in the effective use of rage. Then he saw a man walking across the lot and called out to him. "Hey, Leonard, got a minute?"

He did.

I just wanted to go home.

My scumbag of an agent introduced *that* girl to Leonard Picker and then said, "Oh, and this is Marilee Earle. The afterthought. I don't remember looking him in the eye when we were introduced. We went inside the United Artist wing of the lot and inside a modest office with ordinary furniture and I had to sit there while Beast of an Agent raved about Miss Sexpot.

Mr. Picker said, "I'm sure this young lady is as talented as you say, but you know I don't have anything to do with casting. Why are you telling me this?"

That took Scumbag Agent back for a moment and he sputtered a bit. I heard the nervous laugh and saw Sexpot's smile fade a little. I had the feeling that Leonard was looking at me but I kept my eyes down. I was using all of my energy not to show how humiliated I felt and how angry I was at my agent.

After a few ragged attempts at conversation, Scumbag stood up and thanked Leonard for his time, as Other Girl and I walked with them toward the door. "Just a moment, Marilee." Leonard lightly touched my arm. "Would you stay just a minute, I'd like to talk with you."

"Why?" I asked before I knew what I was saying and it wasn't just the word but the tone in my voice that was rude. I was already humiliated and now…what kind of game was this guy playing? Leonard smiled so sweetly and I knew that

no one with eyes that kind and a voice that tender could possibly be a game player.

"I just want to know why you're so angry."

We were alone then, and I had no intention of telling this man how I felt. But of course I did. There are some people in this world who inspire trust and he was one of those. I talked. He listened. And listened. I remember telling him I didn't want to be an actress anyway, I wanted to be a writer and if people acted this way in show business, I would just as soon go back to my real passion and write a novel.

His dark eyes seemed to look right into my thoughts and he said, "I have to go to a meeting now and this conversation isn't finished—but if you're not busy this evening, I'd like to take you to dinner." There was a pause. "I'm not coming onto you, Marilee, I just like you."

And so it began.

In the weeks and months that followed, we spent so much time together, my parents must have had some concerns about our relationship. Maybe it didn't alarm them because they liked him so much and probably thought my "crush" would surely pass. In the meantime, they had never seen me so happy. Besides they were accustomed to seeing me with people much older than I, so his interest in me might not have seemed unusual.

I had trouble making friends when we moved to California. I was thirteen and felt like I had landed on another planet and I didn't speak the language. My only close friends were my teachers. From my 9th grade English teacher, who asked me to be a bridesmaid in her wedding, or the 10th grade music teacher who took me to the opera because I was determined to see *Aida* and she didn't want me to go alone, to my high school drama coach who offered private acting lessons, or the math teacher who taught me to handicap racehorses on Saturdays, my teen years were not typical.

Long before I was legal age, waiters would ask me if I wanted to order a cocktail. I liked being asked, but wasn't interested in drinking. My parents seemed proud of the fact that I passed as an adult when I was still a kid and I liked it too. I enjoyed the company of their friends and was often included in their social events. I slipped easily into the fascinating world of adults where conversation interested me more than those of my peers.

Leonard talked about subjects I never considered. He took me to movie previews and premiers, parties and concerts. And I loved every glitzy moment of it. But most of all, I loved Leonard. I knew he was much too old for me, but how do you fall out of love, on purpose? Leonard believed in women's rights years before Gloria Steinem was a household name. He hired the first African-American woman to work at United Artists as his secretary. (This was years before that identifying term was created. Even before 'Black' was the proper wording. I think in those days, the politically correct word was 'Colored.') When a waitress wore a nametag, Leonard always made eye contact and called her by her name. He used the same tone of voice when he was talking to the janitor at the studio or the biggest stars in Hollywood. Small moments, but revealing.

Leonard had been divorced twice when we met, and had two daughters, not many years younger than I. A complicated man? Oh, yes he was. He was quick to tell me that he had squandered a great deal of money earlier in his life and when he and his first wife separated, he *"went Hollywood."* He then went on to tell me all the things he did wrong—how he rebelled against his amazing family, enjoyed the pleasures of many women, spent money like it fell from the proverbial trees and how deeply he regretted that his children were caught in the middle of the drama. They had been young when the marital troubles began and naturally, they believed their mother's version of the story. Leonard never defended himself to them and the gossip columnist, Louella Parsons, kept the story alive, fanning the fire in her column. It was terribly painful for his children and for that, Leonard had deep regrets.

What amazed me most was his willingness to let me know his failings, his shadow-side, and to tell me such personal things very early in our relationship. The showing of vulnerability was just not done in the world I knew, where reputation and propriety were so incredibly important and vehemently defended.

It was a long time before I knew that Leonard had once been Howard Hughes' attorney. Years after both of them passed, lawyers wanted to go through boxes of Leonard's papers; they were looking for Howard Hughes' will. (It wasn't there.) It was after his passing that an MCI agent told me that Leonard was the only one who could "handle" both Marilyn Monroe and Frank Sinatra. Whatever that meant.

When Leonard's second oldest daughter, Sue Ann, turned sixteen, she wanted both of her parents and her stepfather, my parents and me, to have dinner together. We went to Trader Vic's at the Beverly Hilton Hotel and I sat across the table from Leonard's first wife. Leonard sat to my left. Actually, it was a lovely evening, and I was fascinated by the conversation. Until his first wife told me, I didn't know that Leonard once owned his own plane and landed it on Harry Cohn's lawn. (How is that possible!) She mentioned that he had trophies from golf competitions and until that moment, I didn't even know that he played. As I said, he was a complicated man.

On the difficult side: Leonard always said exactly what he thought, which was not considered a virtue in my childhood home where diplomacy was admired right along with integrity. Years later, Leonard grumbled when I put Dr. Spock's books about childrearing on the shelf right in the middle of his law books. I remember displeasing him once about some foolish thing and he spoke so harshly I cried, which devastated him and he said, "Oh, darling, don't be sad!" Strong arms wrapped around me. Soft fingers wiped away tears. "Come on now, get dressed! I'm hungry; Are you hungry? Let's go to Chasen's and get some dinner." And so we did.

When we first started going out, it wouldn't have been my parents' style to tell me I couldn't spend so much time with Leonard. Even so, there might have been a bit of manipulation in the gift they offered me for my twenty-first birthday.

A trip to Paris!

I would be traveling alone and didn't know a single person in Paris. I had no job and wasn't going to school. Although I had only been on a plane twice in my life, and that was from Los Angeles to Dallas and back again, I really didn't have much anxiety about traveling by myself. People have told me that it took a lot of courage to take such a trip alone when I was so inexperienced. Actually, it didn't take courage on my part; courage is when you're afraid to do something but you do it anyway. I was fearless in those days and expected only wonderful things to happen. Which they usually did. It's the times that were far less than wonderful that my parents should have been thinking about. They were the ones with courage.

We were not a wealthy family, although we lived graciously. They knew I would be careful about money; I always was. I didn't have a checking account of my own but I was allowed to write on the family checkbook since I was fifteen. Not once did they say I took advantage of their trust.

When I asked my father how much money I could spend in France, he said. "Spend what you need. Don't be extravagant."

It was hard to evaluate how that translated into everyday choices and every day I was in Europe, I worried about it, which wasn't his intention, I'm sure.

When I asked how long I could stay, he said, "We'll see how it goes."

I planned the trip in great detail, designing my journal, creating various organizing systems to make everything work smoothly. Obsessively, I researched where I wanted to stay and what I wanted to see, even assigning certain pockets for dollar bills and others for French francs. My passport must be in a very safe place, deep inside the voluminous handbag I chose for its vast number of compartments. By the time the ship sailed in September, I think I had enough information on France to lead a tour group. Or so my mother said. Her one request was that when I went out with anyone, I would write down that person's name and phone number and leave it on the dresser in my hotel. So, I suppose at some level, she did feel anxious about this trip.

My anxiety wasn't about going to France; it was about leaving Leonard. I didn't need anybody to tell me that it was time to break this off. That didn't stop me from wanting to spend every minute with him. But he had two ex-wives! He had two grown daughters! Of course, I needed to get on with my life. I knew that. Of course I did. The odds were against it ever working out. Spending some time in Paris would help me move on.

It was up to me to plan everything about this trip by myself. It's not that my parents were disinterested, not at all, rather that they had raised me to be resourceful, responsible, and to use good judgment. I was twenty-one and, as they saw it, if they had done their job right, I was ready to leave the nest. That was their philosophy. They loved hearing about my plans but would not make them for me.

Found in Paris

The first lesson on this journey of discovery was that one should not eat a rich pepper steak before boarding a plane for a twelve-hour flight. That's how long it took to fly to New York from Los Angeles in 1955. The rough flight seemed endless and sleep was impossible. I wore a tailored suit with high-heeled shoes and carried my huge handbag. Those were the days ladies dressed up with hats and gloves to ride on airplanes and gentlemen wore suits and ties. This part of the trip was no fun at all. I was incredibly grateful when we finally landed. I would spend one night in New York and then sail on the Liberté to France.

Then came the exhilarating experience of hailing the first cab I ever rode in. The cabby was chatty and told me half his life story before we reached the hotel. So this was New York. Just like I'd seen it in the movies.

One thing I learned from my Great-Aunt Mamie, who was always giving me advice, was that location is everything. "Always go to the best part of town and find the least expensive room. Renting a small room in a respectable neighborhood is better than having spacious quarters in a less desirable part of town."

Weeks before, I had made my reservation in a handwritten letter, requesting the least expensive room at the hotel because I couldn't afford to stay there if it cost too much. Not quite the way we do it these days, is it?

The hotel I chose was the Waldorf Astoria. The cost of their cheapest room was almost twenty dollars and I had the confirmation letter in my purse. The doorman greeted me as if

I was a regular guest in one of the world's greatest hotels. I tried hard not to show that this was one of the most exciting moments of my life. I walked through the grandeur of the lobby and checked in.

When I stepped inside my room, I had the feeling that it was used for something other than guests. It was only large enough for a bed, end table and a lamp. Maybe some kindhearted soul had booked me there just so I could stay at this fabulous hotel. If that was the case, it was just fine with me. And like Great-Aunt Mamie said, this was in a respectable neighborhood.

I worried that I wouldn't hear the alarm clock the next morning and the ship would sail without me, so I didn't sleep much that night. Before dawn, I was up and dressed, on my way to breakfast, and in awe of the grand formality of it. When I saw the menu, I was horrified by the prices and decided that toast and coffee would be quite enough. Then for the first time in my life, I checked out of a hotel. It was an empowering moment and I felt terribly sophisticated. I walked out of the Waldorf, remembering to tip, just as the travel book had instructed me, and discovered that I didn't need to use my newly acquired skill of hailing a cab. The doorman blew his whistle and opened the yellow door to my chariot. I was off for the dock to board the *Liberté* and sail to France.

I wasn't prepared for the size of the ship that looked, of course, like the grand cruise ship that it was, picture-postcard perfect with a black hull and funnels painted red. Oh, that was so French! Just like their flag. I had not the slightest idea where to go or what to do. That didn't matter. I thought I would figure it out as I went along. I just hoped my luggage made it to my cabin because I brought lots of clothes in one trunk-sized suitcase and another small one. My ticket was for Cabin Class; First Class was too expensive and Tourist Class sounded nauseating, down in the bowels of the ship with no air. I had an image of cramped spaces and sweat.

When it was time for dinner, I put on my slinky red satin evening gown that almost touched the floor and headed for the elevator. Leonard was right, why should I eat dinner in Cabin Class, when I could go upstairs and step off into the First Class lounge? Who would stop me? I felt daring and thought I looked so smashingly good in my lovely dress, who would even think of asking if I belonged there?

I was right. I hadn't been in the lounge for long before two middle-aged couples saw that I was alone; they introduced themselves and asked me to join them for dinner. The women wore short cocktail dresses and I thought they hadn't heard about the proper way to dress onboard. I had read that, in First Class, women were to wear long gowns to dinner every night, except on Sundays and for the first night at sea. With that thought, I remembered with a cringe: This *was* the first night at sea! All the women in the room were in short dresses. All except for me.

Well. I took a breath and held my head high, pretending I was the one who was correct and all those other women were just *misinformed!* (Remember this story if you ever think someone is being haughty. It's a sure sign of insecurity.) Dinner was divine, by the way. Conversation was about world affairs, of which I knew little, but I became a fascinated listener. One of the men said he had something to do with NATO; I remember being impressed. The other man was president of Water and Power from a South American country, but I wouldn't tell you which one even if I remembered because later, I'll tell you about *him*.

The music was lovely and I was disappointed that no one asked me to dance. I didn't mind too much though, for people-watching was a sport in itself in that place of entitled gentry, staff, crew and me.

The second night out, I put on a strapless gown of bronze brocade and decided to make more new friends. This was fun.

Of course, in all the excitement of the voyage, I didn't remember that our second night at sea fell on a Sunday. No long gowns on Sunday. So once again I showed up for dinner a little on the overdone side. When you know you're really, really wrong, strike an attitude. I remember telling someone that I always liked to dress for dinner, which was, of course, a flat-out lie.

Crossing the Atlantic took six days and the memories are still vivid, more than half a century later. The seas turned rough and I turned green. It took at least a day to get accustomed to the lunges and the lurches. This time, when I finally made it to dinner, I chose the Cabin Class dining room, where I was supposed to eat, and remembered to wear a simple cocktail dress. Memories rush to mind like snapshots. I see the soup placed before me, the bowl held by some kind of clamping contraption that is supposed to keep it from flying off the table. Suddenly, the ship lunges, the contraption grasps the tabletop and clings to the soup bowl. Nothing however, prevents the pea-green soup from sloshing over the plate and onto the beautiful tablecloth and almost onto me. I decide I'm not hungry tonight.

A few days out to sea, there was an emergency that brought an unexpected drama to the crossing. I felt a change in the way the ship moved and didn't realize that it was slowly coming to a stop. Slowly is the only way a huge vessel can stop, of course, but it made me feel anxious. Once on deck, I saw that there was another boat drifting not far away. People began to gather at the rails. You could feel the concern of the crowd. What was that small boat doing in the middle of the Atlantic Ocean? Of course, small is a relative word. Next to the *Liberté*, almost anything would look small. It seemed like hours before lines were strung between the ships and a hammock-of-sorts was latched to the ropes on the other boat. A report was sent to the passengers: A man was injured and transferring him to the *Liberté* was the fastest way he could get to a hospital in an effort to save his life.

The crowd was silent, watching the man swing wildly above the stormy seas. It was cold on deck and the winds were strong. What was it like for an injured man to be suspended above those dark waters as he was transferred between ships? I wondered if he was conscious and terrified. Did he pray to live, or long to close his eyes and sleep forever in the warm comfort of eternity? Yesterday, he probably felt safe, just going about his life. Maybe that's how everyone lives, thinking they're safe, never knowing what the next day will bring. The cold wind and that sobering thought sent me to my cabin. I would have written about this man in my journal but a migraine headache was in early stages and I had to lie down. I couldn't stop thinking about him, though. I wondered if there was anything the man wished he had said to someone, in case he died.

I made some new friends on the ship, a man from Athens who sang the entire Greek National Anthem one night in the bar. The anthem is very long and his voice was too short for most of the notes. But he tried. And there was a French student who spent some time each day trying to teach me French, horrified by my inability to make my words sound anything like his. (I still had just a tad of a Texas accent.) I told them that just before dawn I was going to the bow of the ship and watch for the first sighting of the lights of France. Watching the sunrise would be magical. They thought so too and planned to meet me, but that was the champagne talking. I was the only one there in the darkness, on the foremost deck, bundled in layers of wool as if this were Antarctica. At last, a few slivers of light broke through the darkness. Then a cluster of lights. There was France, just waking up. It seemed so romantic. I wished I weren't there alone.

Leonard was very much in my thoughts. What would he

have done if I had said, "I've fallen in love with you?" There was no point in thinking about that now. I should stop thinking about him so much. He was too old for me. I knew that.

I arrived in Paris in September of 1955 and stayed at a small hotel just off the Champs-Élysées. The only French I knew were the phrases I learned in the six days I sailed on the *Liberté* crossing the Atlantic. That didn't stop me from blundering ahead the best I could. Sometimes a French person would look amused, others seemed offended, and there were those who pretended not to understand. (At the time, I thought they were pretending, but the odds are they didn't know what on earth I was trying to say.) Still, when I asked a cab driver to take me to Rue de le Paix and he didn't get it until finally, after many attempts on my part, he said, "Alors! Rue de *la* Paix! *La* Paix, Mademoiselle." *La, le*, it was all the same to me at the time and if he had used just a little imagination, I thought he surely could have understood. I was beginning to realize that one should not mess with the French about their language. Never!

Can you imagine—the only large cities I had ever seen were Dallas, Los Angeles, and a quick blink at New York. Oh,—and San Francisco. I modeled swimsuits there at some kind of boat show when I was a teenager. But only for a few days. It's one thing to be watched when you're an actor, something else to be gawked at just because you're in a swim suit. It made me uncomfortable, so I left. In any case, I had a rather limited view of the world and then, that September, there was Paris.

I had never seen anything like that before in all my life. Like many who came before me, I sort of felt like I had discovered it and never wanted to let it go. If I slip back in memory to all those years ago, I can feel the heartbeat of Paris: the Seine carving a moat around the city, real gold on the curls of buildings, artists and lovers living free and wild. Life was happening on those streets and I was determined to be part of it. I wanted to be more than a tourist. Somehow I heard about *Alliance Francaise* and signed up for French lessons. After buying numerous books, I must have thought I could learn by osmosis, just patting them, stacking them, opening and closing them, putting them under my pillow. Alas, it was not to be. Even now, I speak abominable tourist French.

The next few days were spent trying to figure out how to use the Metro, where to change dollars into francs, and how to avoid being killed by speeding traffic in a city that apparently had no rules of order. Or simply didn't care.

After a few days in a hotel I set out to find a more affordable place to live. Great-Aunt Mamie's voice tickled my ear. *"Location is everything."* A lawyer and his family advertised a room and private bath for rent in their apartment so I went to check it out. The address was *Quatre-vingt-dix-huit Rue de Miromesnil*. It was an 18th Century building in the *8th Arrondissement*. I fell in love with the elevator made of glass and iron, although it moved so slowly I could have gotten to the third floor faster by taking the stairs. The door to the apartment opened and I saw a tall, stately woman who looked at me as if she had X-ray eyes and could see right into my character. I gave her my most sincere ingénue smile and stepped into a vaulted entry with Louis XIV furnishings and an enormous crystal chandelier. How could this possibly be cheap? Maybe I misread the paper.

Madame spoke very little English and I used up all my French words even before she led me down a long dimly lit hallway to a tiny bedroom. It was only large enough for a bed, a small dresser and an armoire where I could hang a few of my clothes. I could barely turn around without bumping into the furniture. But where would I put my enormous suitcase? Then Madam opened the door to a huge bathroom with a tall ceiling. A claw-foot tub faced a lovely fireplace. It also had a bidet where I could shave my legs. The toilet was down the hall.

I think the room used to be the maid's quarters for it was separate from the rest of the very large apartment. I had every intention of staying for quite a while. It didn't matter that I wasn't allowed to enter the living room or the kitchen or any part of this grand apartment except the hallway that led off the entry to my bedroom.

The best part was that it was cheaper than a hotel and I could rent it by the month. It was clean and warm. And, of course it was in the perfect part of town.

Before leaving Los Angeles, I had an appointment with Paul Kohner at his international talent agency on Sunset Blvd. Why this fine agent accepted me as a client when I had so few acting credits is still a mystery. He arranged an interview for me in Paris with the director of *The Ambassador's Daughter*, Norman Krasna. The film had a terrific cast: Olivia de Havilland, John Forsythe, Edward Arnold, Adolph Menjou, Myrna Loy and Tommy Noonan. (You may be too young to know those names but they were major movie stars in those days.)

I was so excited, I hardly closed my eyes the night before. When I finally met Norman Krasna, my audition lasted about three minutes. I had only two words to say in the film but they were in French: *"Taffetas, Monsieur."* I said them twice, in a Marilyn Monroe kind of voice, years before she made the style famous. I got the part.

Filming wouldn't start until November and I had to be available for fittings in October. It is truly possible to walk across a room without ever touching the floor, buoyed by nothing but pure joy.

*****

A few weeks later, I was settling into Paris, doing the things that tourists do, falling in love with the Seine, the architecture, the music of the language, the taste of the food. Then I was invited to join my Aunt Winifred and Uncle Joe in Venice where they were vacationing. They would rent a car and we would drive to Rome. After that, they would drive me back to Paris before they flew home to Dallas. Well, why not? I was planning to be in Paris a very long time. And it would be great to see Italy.

I took the night-train to Venice and a boat to the hotel where Winifred and Joe were staying. It's exciting to be twenty-one, even better to know that somehow you can find your way around without a map, without knowing the language, without having a friend to support you.

On the road between Venice and Rome, how many museums and ancient churches do you think there are? A hundred? A thousand? I would have bet there were even more and I saw the insides of every one of them on our journey south. How I longed to spend time at the street markets and to have a little time by myself. But after they saw a guy in Venice pinch my bummy they would not let me out of their sight.

Italians love their street-side cafes and they certainly are charming. But I'm allergic to bees and my Aunt Winifred was terrified of cats. If there's anything that Italy has more of than anywhere else in the world, I'm sure it's hungry bees and homeless cats. They were everywhere. Uncle Joe was a patient man, but it couldn't have been easy for him.

Once in Rome, I had business to attend to with my agent's representative and they had no choice but to let me out of their clutches. They were in love with the history of Rome and spent every moment in cultural pursuits; I was in love with the shops and the language and the cafes. Mostly, I was excited about meeting an agent from the Rome office of the

Paul Kohner Agency. Maybe I could get a role in an Italian film, after I finished work in Paris. I was not lacking in confidence.

There was a long wait in Paul Kohner's office and a handsome Italian actor and I began to talk. I didn't mind the wait at all, especially when this gorgeous man invited me to dinner and then to go dancing. This sounded much more interesting than having dinner with my aunt and uncle who would be making plans for yet one more museum tour.

I'm not sure what happened that night that made this actor feel the need to 'defend my honor' as he put it. It had something to do with the way I danced. In any case, he told me that it was necessary for him to tell the offending man who joined our table at a nightclub that I was his cousin from America. Well, if I were his cousin, that would mean that I was a *Contessa*, and since he was quite proud of his ancestral lineage, the story took off from there.

I had no idea that the rumor would start about me in Rome and make its way to Paris and onto the set of *The Ambassador's Daughter*. No matter what Myrna Loy may have told you, if you were in Paris in 1955—I am not and never was a *Contessa*; I did not come from great wealth; my parents did not send me to Europe to keep me from a man they were afraid I would marry. (At least, I don't think they did.)

When I was back in Paris and on the set of *The Ambassador's Daughter*, I met Myrna Loy. She gave me her dazzling movie star smile and the first thing she said to me was, "Is your coat *really* lined in mink?"

What do you say to that! Something like: *"No ma'am, my mother made my coat and I think it's lined in flannel?"* It was quite a while before I learned the origin of the rumor. Hollywood is not just a place in California, it's a village with clusters all over the planet and gossip travels fast in the film community. So I, who had never made one single movie, and would only say two words in this one, quite suddenly had a glamorous reputation.

When I wrote my parents I thought they would think it was as funny as I did, but I received a letter telling me that I must correct that story immediately. "You wouldn't want anyone to get the wrong impression about you."

I wouldn't? Why not? Actually, I thought it was a delightful idea and so long as I didn't say the words myself, I felt no obligation to say, "No, I'm not a *Contessa*; I'm just a college drop out, with no history of royalty that I know of, and I'm spending as little money as possible so I can stay in Paris as long as I can."

Oh, I think not.

The rumor spread, as rumors are wont to do. One night when I walked into Maxim's famous restaurant with my dinner date I saw one of the stars of *The Ambassador's Daughter*, Adolph Menjou, sitting at his table at the back of the room. He stood and raised his glass of champagne for a toast. In his suave, projected voice he announced to the room: "La Belle de Paris!"

I looked behind me to see who that belle was—and then I realized: his tribute was to me. If anything was undeserved, this was it, but do you think I treasured this moment? Oh, my goodness yes! We are talking about phony fame, built on nothing but rumor, undeserved, unwarranted in every way. I had done nothing to earn applause, but in grand Hollywood style, I received it. Did I think I was practicing for my soon-to-be-Academy Award? Basking in the hot light of undeserved celebrity, I played the role to the hilt. But back in my little room in the former servants quarters on *Rue de Miromesnil*, what I really felt was that I was somehow a fraud. My mother was right; I should have told them it wasn't true. I really wasn't a *Contessa*.

I raise my right hand, place the other on the Bible. I am telling you the absolute truth. In fiction, one wouldn't dare write this next story. But this is real life and this is what happened:

It was the first day of the month and my rent was due. The sky was threatening to storm and I was anxious to get to the bank and back to my apartment before the heavens broke. With flat-heeled shoes and a scarf over my hair, tied like a Russian babushka, I went to my bank on the Champs-Élysées. As I walked out, a man touched my arm and said, "Excuse me, aren't you Marilee Earle?"

I stared at him. How could this man possibly know my name?

He smiled, "I'm Joe Schoenfeld, Editor of *Variety*. I interviewed you in Los Angeles, several months ago."

I was too embarrassed to even remember what I said but I can't imagine that it was clever. He invited me for a coffee and now I tried to interview him. "Where were you going on this dreary day?" And here's the unbelievable part...he said, "I'm going to meet Norman Krasna; he's making a film here in Paris. I was just going to take a cab to the studio."

So of course, I said I had a part in the film. No, I didn't tell him it was just two words. Then he asked me if I'd come with him to the set. The hardest acting part I ever played was a girl trying not to look ecstatic and unsophisticated. This man was a film critic. It's hard to fool the good ones. It's a long cab ride out of the heart of the city and to the studio. By the time we arrived, we had exchanged the headlines of our life stories.

Walking onto the set of *The Ambassador's Daughter* with the Editor of Variety certainly added to the fable that had already spun around me. Was it fun to have lunch with the director, the critic, and Tony Curtis, who just happened to be making a picture on another set? Was it unbelievably fascinating to join Norman Krasna and his wife for cocktails at their home and then dinner at La Tour D'Argent with Joe and a handful of actors and writers? Joe stayed in Paris for several days and asked me to go with him to all the fascinating places, with all the interesting people that were on his schedule. When I returned to California, Joe and his wife, Edna, met Leonard and me for dinner. We became such close friends that they visited me at the hospital years later when Gina was born and even came to her baptism.

There is more to tell about the man I met in Rome, the Italian actor-turned-defender-of-women. He said his last name was Medici, which could very well just have been a stage name. I certainly didn't assume it had anything to do with *the* Medici family that dated back to the 12th Century and were major players in the Renaissance. But I did check the phone book and found numerous listings for the name Medici. On the next evening, we had dinner with some of his friends and then all of us went back to his house for an after-dinner drink. I had never seen a house so enormous with such magnificent antiques in all the limited experience of my twenty-one years. We were joined by a fashion model from Balenciaga, who was painfully skinny and only spoke Italian and French, and another couple who spoke only Italian and my host who spoke all three languages. And there I was, not understanding a word the other guests said.

There are not many things you can say at a party when you only have a vocabulary of about fifty French words and lack the ability to conjugate verbs. And even my fifty words were about how to rent a room and order dinner. Hardly fascinating conversation.

Soon, my new friend got tired of translating and I was beginning to think my aunt and uncle were probably having a better time. Before the evening ended, a butler brought a rare port from the cellar. It was more than a hundred years old and the liquid gold was poured for each of us in tiny crystal glasses. It tasted nasty to my uneducated taste buds but I really never meant to make a terrible face when I took a small sip. With a scowl, our host took the glass from me and poured what remained of my port back in the bottle. He said something in Italian and the others laughed. I longed to be back at the hotel. But as fate would have it, there was one more *faux pas* I was to make before leaving Rome.

I was invited to lunch by Roberto Haggag, who was a friend of Leonard's. It was a very formal setting and I was remembering to hold my fork in my left hand in the upside down way of European custom and not to transfer it to my right. When the fruit course arrived, I took the serving spoon and fork from the plate held by the waiter on my left and transferred a luscious pear onto my fruit plate. Roberto sat on my right, charming me with his lovely Italian accent. He kept me amused all through lunch. I felt quite at ease, even if he was the head of United Artists in Italy. Another man, who was quite serious, sat across from me and if he spoke English, he kept that knowledge to himself.

In Europe, fruit is always peeled with a knife and fork and when you carve a bit for yourself it is so that the skin never touches your lips. I practiced every night at dinner on the *Liberté*—only the fruit of choice on the ship was peaches, which are much softer than pears. I learned to peel peaches rather well—you would never have known that in Texas, I grew up holding a peach in my hand and taking large bites of the juicy stuff with hardly any of it dripping on my chin. But this was not Dallas, it was Rome; this was not a peach, this was a pear, a pear that was hard as a baseball. When I, oh so carefully, stabbed it with my fork to hold it steady as I cut into it with the knife, the damned thing leapt from my plate as if it were alive, under attack, and running as fast as it could to get away from my fruit knife. Then it bounced several times on the inlaid table rolling right onto the plate of the oh-so-serious man seated across from me. He looked appalled by my incompetence. Roberto laughed so hard you could have heard him in China. I tried to pretend it was just a funny little thing that I had learned to do, but I could feel a hot flush in my cheeks and really, there was nothing I could say or do that would make me look less like an absolute klutz.

*****

Do you remember the two couples who invited me to dinner on the *Liberté*? They were so charming when my aunt and uncle and I ran into them near the Spanish Steps in Rome. They seemed pleased that I had a part in a movie and would be staying in Paris for a while. "Will you join us for dinner when we return?" one of them asked and oh, you bet I would. I gave them my new landlady's phone number and looked forward to a scrumptious meal in a great restaurant with interesting people, sometime in November.

Back in Paris, it was time for my fitting at Christian Dior's. That in itself would have been worth the ticket abroad. I walked in wearing a dress my mother designed and made and overheard a salesgirl say, "*La robe est tres jolie!*" I couldn't wait to write my mother and tell her that her couturier skills were appreciated, even at Dior's.

My first fitting was for a fabulous red taffeta cocktail dress that I would wear in the scene with Olivia de Havilland and John Forsythe. It was not only gorgeous and sophisticated, it was the most complicated design I had ever seen on a dress. Then there was the fitting for the bridesmaid dress that I would wear at Olivia's wedding. (I didn't call her Olivia to her face.) There was another session with a famous hair stylist who showed only disdain for my long dark hair and immediately cut it short. I did not cry. Then he wanted to make me a blonde and I absolutely refused. I thought the only good thing about my hair was the color and I was getting my moxie back. "No!" I demanded and he looked shocked. It's a good thing I didn't know enough French to tell him what I was really thinking. He backed off with a huff and saying things that it's just as well I couldn't translate. Probably called me a spoiled American. I didn't care.

On the day of the first shoot, the studio sent a car to pick me up. I didn't expect that, and was surprised that saying two words in the scene earned such attention. It was still dark outside and the studio was a long way from the center of Paris. Only later did it occur to me that they were protecting themselves from a no-show. There would not be a car to take me home at the end of the day.

This was my first experience on a movie set. It wasn't going to be the last. The scene played well, and I got my two words right on the first take. The actors were friendly and I was in heaven.

Why didn't I ask someone for a ride back to town? It never occurred to me to ask. Everyone was going that way but since no one offered to take me, I found my way to the Metro and bought a ticket back to Paris. A long time later, it looked like the next stop would be my station. I quickly got off the Metro. The train pulled away and I knew it was the wrong place. No one else was there and I didn't know where to wait for the next train. There was no ticket booth. Maybe someone would be outside. I climbed the stairs. No, I was alone. This was a residential neighborhood. I walked around looking for signs I might be able to read. There were none. A man was walking toward me and I asked him where to catch the Metro for Paris. He didn't understand what I was saying and with a shrug he walked on. It was dark now and cold.

So many years later, I am writing this but as hard as I try, I cannot remember how I got home. There are many techniques one can use to stimulate memory but none are working now. I don't know what I did. Did someone finally show me how to get back on the proper Metro line? I remember the lonely street as only residential buildings, and no cabs. Did I have money for a cab even if I found one? This is most disturbing. But it's better to leave this story without a conclusion, than to make something up. Somehow I got home.

It was weeks later when, once again, a car arrived to take me to the location for the day's shoot. It was the wedding scene and we were standing outside a church in a scene that required many takes and lots of time waiting around. I was wearing a Christian Dior gown: a white silk bridesmaid's dress that was sleeveless and had a plunging neckline. It was already well into December. We stood there for hours, one take after another in the freezing cold. They were shooting 'winter for spring' but I thought for sure my goose bumps would show in the film.

On breaks, a nearby bar was the only place actors could go and we stayed warm by huddling around the fire and drinking cognac. It was the first time I ever tasted brandy. The liquid burned my tongue but it did make me feel warmer. It didn't do my body much good however, because I spent Christmas in the hospital with my lungs aching from pleurisy.

When the movie opened in LA, I was so proud of myself you would have thought it was a real part and not just a walk-on. At least it was called a "major motion picture," and I thought it was a wonderful film. (Particularly the eight seconds in which I got a close-up.) But last year I got a copy of the movie on Ebay and I must tell you it was the silliest premise and the most ridiculous movie you would ever see. I didn't even save it for my grandchildren. The dresses were really lovely however, and I could have purchased either of the original Christian Dior gowns that I wore in the film for seventy-five American dollars. I thought that was much too much money to spend on a dress when my mother made such pretty ones, so I didn't buy either one.

When I married Leonard, she even made my wedding gown, based on a design I remembered from Dior's. I sketched it when I got out of the salon and since my mother never needed a pattern for a gown, she made it perfectly from my drawing. Inset panels of lace in *peau de soir* with pearls embedded in the lace all the way down the long train. *Oh, la la;* it was *magnifique!* I had the gown preserved for my daughters to wear when they married. But later, it burned in the Bel Air fire.

*****

There's more about the couples I met on the *Liberté* and then again in Rome. Well, shortly after I returned to Paris, one of the men called and asked if I could join them for dinner the following evening. We were to meet in the lounge of the George V Hotel, which was/is one of the most luxurious hotels in Paris. I put on one of the beautiful dresses my mother designed and arrived right on time.

We had an aperitif in the lounge, and I kept wondering why their wives were so late. Then the check was signed and it was time to go to dinner. "Where are your wives?" I asked.

"Oh, they went to the Opera."

I didn't know what to say to that. I didn't think I should be going out to dinner with two married men but they acted like it was nothing improper and frankly, I just didn't want to be rude and had no idea the polite way to say I shouldn't join them.

We went to a place on the Left Bank, to a restaurant that looked like a cave, all beautiful white stones, steps that led down and then further down. There was music. It was beautiful. I wished their wives had come, and I didn't know why these men hadn't chosen a night when all of us would have been together. They ordered champagne and poured some for me. I went to the restroom and when I returned, I sipped my drink.

The champagne didn't taste right. I didn't want to complain. I sipped again. Something was definitely wrong—not that I was any connoisseur. There was something about the way they watched me that made me uncomfortable. I wished I had never come with them. Sometimes you know something but you don't want to know that you know. Finally, when I knew I couldn't/shouldn't drink the stuff in front of me, I said, "Don't you think there's something wrong with this champagne?"

It was the quick look they exchanged that confirmed what I was thinking. I knew I was in trouble. I had to get out of there but once again I didn't know what to say. Clutching my purse, I just ran from the table, out the door and into a cab that was parked outside. I gave the driver my address, hoping I could get back to my apartment before the strange feeling worsened. I was dizzy. Once in my bed the effects were strong and frightening. The room seemed to rock. I had trouble moving my head. Suddenly, I felt numb and very sleepy. The next morning I was still feeling strange.

In today's world, any girl with half a brain would know right away that her drink had been drugged. But I was doubting myself and hoping that maybe I was wrong about them. Maybe one would call the next day to say that they also had a terrible night and were very sick and why did I run away? The champagne must have gone bad, I wanted to hear them say. Of course they didn't call. Weeks later, I saw them at the Opera; when I made eye contact with one of them, he looked alarmed and they disappeared in the crowd.

There were so many times I could have gotten into serious trouble in Europe. Those who don't believe in angels have attributed this story to my well-developed sense of intuition. Maybe they're right. Or maybe that's just how angels work. I really don't know.

There was one thing about this trip that was quite revealing. In spite of the excitement and the fascinating people, the career opportunities that were offered, (one was to make a film in Spain) I missed Leonard terribly.

Six months after I arrived in Paris, I flew home.

Shifting Goals

When I returned from Paris, Leonard and my parents met me at the airport. I had stayed in touch with him through letters but I wondered if there was a woman in his life. He hadn't said there was, so that was encouraging. From the moment I passed through customs and his arms wrapped around me, I knew that he had missed me more than he said in his letters. It wasn't easy for him to let me go. He pulled away, then pulled me toward him. It was a lover's embrace. Sometimes absence does let the heart see clearly. He was much too old for me. I didn't care. My parents did, however. I saw a look between them that meant something was not right. At that time, Leonard had said nothing about a long-term relationship.

We went to a friend's wedding, which might have started that conversation, but it didn't. I did meet another man who kept watching me throughout the reception. Leonard went to get us drinks when the man came over and introduced himself. He was a producer, ready to shoot a film in New York.

"You're an actress, aren't you?"

I gave him my most perfected smile. And wasn't I glad I'd worn my hair up with a cocktail hat I bought in Paris and a dress my mother made that was drop dead gorgeous?

"A good one?" he teased.

"Of course!" I said.

"You have the perfect look for one of the models, do you want to read for the part? It's a small role, but...hey."

"I'm not afraid of small roles. I just came back from Paris

and I had a small part in the Krasna film." I didn't say it was only two words. "Is it an interesting character?"

This is how it goes in Hollywood. This is the game. He dangled the part; I showed interest. Both of us knew I was dying to take it but we played by the rules. "I'll send you the script. Then we'll see."

I read the script and was disappointed. It wasn't just a small part, it was a dull part. There was, however, another role. It was an ingénue role that was sassy and fun with lots of scenes where I could really show off a bit. I had a plan.

A few days later, I auditioned and got the part the producer had in mind. (Anybody could have, for it required no talent at all.) The part was so small the director didn't even have to approve it. Then I asked if I could read for the ingénue part. He turned me down. "The director's in New York and he'd have to make that decision—it's a major part. Anyway, you're much too sophisticated for that role."

"But I'm an actress," I said. "How about this—I'll accept the part you offered me, but I'll pay my own way to New York and audition for the part of Nancy. If the director says 'no', it's no problem. I'll stay there and play the model. You won't have to pay for my ticket. If he says 'yes', and I get to play Nancy, I don't care who pays for the ticket!"

He had a great laugh. It had an '*I gotcha*' sound to it. "That's a deal. Who's your agent? I can't wait to hear what he says about that!"

I didn't care what they paid me or even *if* they paid me, I got my card for the Screen Actor's Guild and I was sure I'd get the part of Nancy.

Days later in New York, I met with the director, William Burke. I wore my hair in a ponytail, a pink cashmere sweater, flat shoes and a sassy attitude. I read for the part and got it. Nancy was mine! Bill said, "I don't know why Phil ever thought you could play the model. You're much too young for that part!"

The film was called "Street of Sinners" and George

Montgomery was the lead actor. Geraldine Brooks was in it too. The title sounds raunchy but in today's world, it would have had a G rating. The part was fun but it really was just a B film.

The important part of the trip was that I met Leonard's mother and adored her. She invited me to lunch and then asked my intentions with her son. I told her I would marry him if he asked me but didn't know if he would. Now how's that for a start of a relationship!

She wanted me to meet Leonard's oldest brother, Eugene, and his family. The next night, she picked me up at the hotel after I got in from location. She had a gift for me. It was a triple-strand pearl bracelet with a beautiful heart-shaped ruby clasp. I guess I passed the test.

There was just one thing. Mrs. Picker wasn't too happy that I wasn't Jewish. My parents only worried about Leonard's age, not his heritage. But there was an alleged friend in Dallas who said to me, "If you marry that man, you'll never be able to join the country club."

"Neither will Jesus," I told her.

So there were a few obstacles to overcome. The first of course, was that Leonard still hadn't asked me to marry him. I knew he had only dated women closer to his age and that the years between us bothered him more than they did me. He loved me, that was clear, but he was thinking of my life in years to come. I wanted children. (That concerned his mother, but not him.)

"Do you *want* to marry me?" he asked.

"Yes. Is that a proposal?" I answered. He was flustered.

"Darling, I am very much in love with you but I've been divorced twice. I'm not an easy man to live with. And I have grown daughters. I'm scared to death!"

"I'm not."

"Thank God you haven't just set a deadline and said for me to take it or leave it!"

I didn't say a word.

"Have you?" He looked worried.

I smiled and said, "Let's see how it goes."

A few weeks later, I said 'yes' to his sweet proposal and we made plans for the wedding.

When my father pointed out that while the age gap made no difference now, in time it would be a problem. I remember saying, "Well, I can be happy now or I can be happy later. I choose now."

After all those years of my parents training me to think for myself, they couldn't change the rules at this point.

On the day we married, Leonard and I had known each other for almost three years. Our wedding was in Dallas, where most of my family lived. It was a small wedding in the SMU Methodist chapel and my bridesmaids were girls I'd gone to grade school with. My parent's friends (whom I always considered my friends, as well) were there also, and apparently charmed by this charismatic man who lived in a world far from their own.

Mother Picker wanted us to be married by a rabbi and I thought that was a great idea. Two weddings were fine with me and I didn't care who married us first. I'll take all the blessings I can get. The problem was that we couldn't find a rabbi who would marry us since I wasn't going to convert. So, one wedding was all we had. Mother Picker was okay with that. She came down from New York, with Leonard's brother, Arnold and his wife Ruth. Eugene couldn't make the wedding.

I'll never forget Arnold's words as he lifted his glass of champagne to me: "The last toast I made was to the Queen of England. This one gives me even greater pleasure."

Our honeymoon was in Nassau. Why Nassau, you may wonder? Well. The reason is a bit strange. We had originally planned to go to Hawaii. We'd made all the arrangements, then I got an offer to play opposite Vince Edwards (remember Dr. Ben Casey?) in a calypso musical to be shot in the Bahamas. The director was Bill Burke, who directed that movie I made months ago in New York. Of course, I turned it down. It was scheduled to start the week after our wedding. How can a bride spend her honeymoon playing love scenes with another man!

When I told Leonard, he said, "Why would you turn it down? We can cancel Hawaii and honeymoon in Nassau. This is a good role for you. Call your agent back and say you'll take it! We have years ahead of us so don't throw this away." As you may already have realized, ours was not a conventional marriage.

It was a wonderful honeymoon and great fun to work on a film with my brand new husband by my side. He did say one thing that I didn't like. The first morning when I heard that the woman doing my makeup would come to our room after she finished making up Marie Windsor, I said, "Oh, I'll just go down to her room, then she won't have to set up everything twice."

"You'll never be a movie star, Marilee."

"Why not!"

"You don't have the ego for it. Makeup people come to you, you don't go to them." Then he whispered, "That's one of the reasons I love you."

I wasn't ready to give up on my career. A few months later, I had a minor part in a western starring Sterling Hayden. I played Sebastian Cabot's mistress in Terror in a Texas Town; it was shot in Hollywood and I was only on the set for a few days. Even so, it was one more credit.

Five months after we were married, I became pregnant and happier than I'd ever been in my life. The day after the doctor confirmed our good news, I had a part on a TV show, The Life of Riley. William Bendix, the star of the show, asked me when my due date was. How could he know! We hadn't told anyone yet. I was skinny as a bean with a concave tummy. How could he possibly know! I asked him and I love the answer he gave: "I can see it in your eyes."

I was busy moving into our new home, trying to learn to cook (which I did badly) and entertaining interesting people (which I did well). One night, when we had a dinner party for eight in our home in the Hollywood Hills, one of the guests was Joe Schoenfeld, my editor friend from Paris. The dining table was beautifully set but the meat was so rare, it was like taking a bite out of the cow. With a twinkle in his eye, Joe said, "Marilee, if you were my wife, I wouldn't let you near the kitchen!"

I was reading every childrearing book I could get my hands on and I stopped taking acting lessons from Estelle Harman. Acting was fun, but it was no longer my passion. Even writing wasn't on my mind.

I made two more films before Gina was born at St. John's Hospital in Santa Monica. At barely four months pregnant, I played the romantic lead opposite Dana Andrews in a propaganda anti-communist film that would put even Dana's best fans to sleep. When the filming ran past schedule, and I was obviously pregnant, my expanding tummy won me close-ups for the last few weeks of shooting. There was nothing we could do about my chubby chipmunk cheeks in the middle of my fifth month.

Then Bill Burke called again and wanted me to play a pregnant woman in a science fiction film with Robert Logia. So, when I was eight months pregnant, I played a woman giving birth as the world was on the brink of destruction. Oh, I had no idea! Just a little huff and puff and out pops baby? Oh, I think not. Too bad they didn't film this after I had a little experience in the delivery room.

*****

I had emotionally detached from my acting career even before my baby was born. Nothing could have been more satisfying than holding little Gina in my arms and seeing my husband's adoration of this six pound two ounce wonder. Leonard bragged about how beautiful she was and he was convinced that during the five days we were in the hospital, she had wrapped the nurses around her wee fingers and was the star player in the nursery. She was a charmer, even then.

Hospital food being what it was, Leonard came to my room every night bearing special meals from Chasen's Restaurant. No wine, of course, for I was nursing my baby, but fabulous food. That man really did have style.

A few months later, I interviewed for a part in a new TV series and I was a serious contender for the role. Then I heard that the series would be made in San Francisco! At that moment, I said I didn't want the part. I had a family to take care of. The director said, "Well, your husband can come up on weekends and you can get a nurse for your baby."

Suddenly, everything became absolutely clear to me. I didn't have my baby to leave her with a nanny. It was very easy to walk away from that career. I don't criticize others who would have made a different decision. I just knew what was right for me and I never had another interview again.

Maybe I would start writing again later, but in 1958, life with my family was all I needed.

Two and a half years later, when Tamara was born at Cedar's Sinai, fathers were not allowed in the labor rooms, and certainly not in the delivery room. But Leonard somehow got into the doctor's dressing room and borrowed a surgical gown, cap and mask. He slipped in unnoticed and stayed with me for the longest time until someone discovered him and he was promptly evicted with stern warnings about breaking the rules. He was so enchanted by Tamara, the little one who was born breach and therefore came into the world pale as a Christmas angel and blonde as hair can be. I can still hear the awe in his voice when he whispered, "Isn't she just so beautiful!" He was devoted to both of his girls.

About a month after Leonard died, his youngest brother, Arnold, heard that I was planning to use the insurance money from our destroyed home to buy a house. He flew from New York and sat me down for the "Big Brother" talk. He was patient but firm: "You don't want to be tied down now and you certainly don't need the responsibilities of a house!" I didn't understand his kind of reasoning. He didn't understand mine. I didn't grow up in New York City where most people live in apartments or condos; I grew up in Dallas where, if you were an adult and had any financial resources at all, you bought a house. End of story. A house had meaning far deeper than shelter and comfort, it was something that tethered you to stability and even the fire had not destroyed my illusion that a house provided security.

I was much younger than the four brothers in the Picker family, and much less knowledgeable about money than any of them. I knew absolutely nothing about the stock market and even less about bonds. I understood emotional needs but that carried no weight at all in this conversation. I had no training in finances but Arnold was Vice President of United Artist. So I listened. I might have been naïve but I wasn't stupid. The Picker family was a powerful force in the motion picture business. Leonard's father, who emigrated from Russia, started in the movie business by owning a Nickelodeon in the Bronx and then owned thirteen theaters; in 1913, he became a partner in Loew's theaters as their companies merged. Later, Eugene was president of Transamerica. He agreed with Arnold. This family understood money. Leonard let it slip through his fingers in his early years. He was the playful one in the family. He only became a lawyer because of a promise he made to his father on his death bed. Being a motion picture lawyer turned out to be a good thing, however, and he never regretted it.

"Marilee, you need to think about your future," Arnold said firmly. "You're young and you have to get on with your life."

Eugene said, "You'll meet someone and, well...we're going to hear a lot of stories and we're not going to believe any of them. You find yourself a good man. Okay?"

How could he possibly think that I could just...*find* another man! After *Leonard?* I was appalled by the very idea. I insisted I never would get married again. He just smiled.

I couldn't rebuild my home but I didn't have to stay in that house where Leonard died. That place where we had no history but pain, no memories that comforted. My mother, the girls and I, were settling into a routine in a house we rented in Sherman Oaks, furnished with the things I moved from a mountain cabin my dad built in Squaw Valley, now listed for sale.

Weeks passed, then months. My days revolved around my children. I was making them the center and the periphery of my life, which is an emotional burden that children should never have to carry. The world I was creating was too small to be healthy for any of us.

Then Leonard's mother called from New York. She had obviously been talking with Eugene. "It's time you started looking around a bit, Sweetie. You are much too young to be staying at home all the time. Leonard would want you to start going out. You know that. Now use your eyes, Marilee."

Grief takes its time and cannot be rushed but behavior can be changed, once you make up your mind. I had lost my dreams but the sooner I made new ones, the better life would be for my girls and for me. My head knew that but my heart was resisting. Still, I had to admit that the walls were beginning to close in on me a bit. It had been five months since Leonard died. It would be good to just go out to dinner with an interesting man, or to a screening, or perhaps to a dinner party where I didn't have to go alone.

I needed something to look forward to. So I went to a fabric store, where I bought yards of exquisite taffeta brocade. My mother designed clothes that could hold their own with the finest couturier, but she only sewed for herself and for me. I spread the brocade across the bed. It was spectacular. "I want to go to the Academy Awards," I told her. "Will you make the dress?" For the last six years, Leonard and I had always gone to the Awards. He was West Coast Counsel for United Artists and our lives spun around the events of "The Industry." I remembered the ritual: the long elegant gown, the upswept hair, the white kid gloves stretched tight to the elbow, the limousine that pulled up to the red carpet before the excited crowd. There were always parties, grand celebrations and in those days United Artists was the Alpha in the room. There were stars and I was starry-eyed. My excitement always amused Leonard, who saw the evening as just part of his job.

I knew so many people in the film business—surely one of them would invite me. Attending the Academy Awards would mean I was still part of that fascinating world, still the woman I was before Leonard died. I thought I still belonged in that world. I did not.

The awards came and went and I watched them on TV, just like most people did. Reality was setting in. No matter what I wanted, I was no longer part of the film industry. There were many places I no longer belonged.

If I had reached out to friends, perhaps the story would have been different. Would it have been so wrong to tell people how much that evening symbolized to me? How desperately I needed community and to feel that this industry, this unique creative family that was a container for such a large part of my identity, had not disowned me?

What a naïve perception that was! But this story is about

telling the truth and that's how it seemed to me at the time. I probably could have gone to the awards, if I had just told someone at United Artists how much it meant to me. But that would mean asking for help, which wasn't in my upbringing. Just like it never occurred to me that I could have asked Leonard's family if they would be there for me financially, if the time came that I needed it. Even when I worried about money, and what I would do when it was gone, I knew I would never ask.

Leonard and I had always entertained at Chasen's Restaurant, and we were there for dinner about twice a week. It was the place to be in the 50's and 60's. We were always seated at the second booth on the left. Sometimes it was the third booth, if a higher-ranking Hollywood personality showed up first. Then one night in February, I went there with an old friend and the maître d' who had seated Leonard and me night after night for years, looked right through me. My friend and I were seated far in the back, in a room I didn't even know existed. I did not belong, even there. I had become invisible.

Years later, I told this story to Ron Field, a choreographer of many Broadway shows, who won five Tony awards and two Emmy's. He didn't understand why I was so upset by an obvious rule of life in Hollywood that was no different than Broadway: "Well, of course he didn't seat you in your old booth. The booth is his showcase. Only people who are important get to sit there. I wouldn't even think of going to Sardi's if I didn't have a hit show on Broadway!"

I felt foolish to have let such a superficial rejection become just one more reinforcement of my separation from the world I loved. It wasn't about restaurants or prestige; it was just a curt reminder that nothing would ever be the same.

Leonard's mother was wonderful to me, she wrote beautiful letters and called often. She was a stunning seventy-five year old woman with thick white hair, olive skin, large expressive eyes and a manner that demanded attention. Regal and powerful, she was quite magnificent. If she walked into a restaurant with Sophia Loren, I think all eyes would have been on Mother Picker. This phrase always comes to mind: *"She is the stuff that queens are made of."*

She said, "So, have you met any single men?" I had not. She was not pleased. Was I even trying to meet someone? I said I wasn't ready. "You won't be ready until you put yourself out there." I didn't know how to do that or even where to begin.

I knew she was right and I knew I had to let go and move on. She just didn't know how hard this was. The voices around me and inside my head pushed me out my door, insisting that the longer it was before I dated, the harder it would be.

It wasn't long after our conversation that I did meet a man, and then another. I wasn't attracted to either of them but they were *there*, they were single, and they were attentive. One was a friend of a friend. The other was a man I met at an art gallery on a Sunday afternoon. I welcomed the evenings out but it was hard work to have meaningless conversations. Sometimes I would go in the ladies room, dab a towel with cold water and hold it to my temples, reminding myself that it was important to try. Obviously, no sparks were flying. I just wanted to go home to my children and sleep through the night, to rest in a dreamless sleep.

The men were nice enough but dull and when I spoke of them to my mother, I called them, rather unkindly, Frick and Frack—not that they were funny or that they even knew each other—but those names came from a world that had nothing to do with mine. As did those two men.

It wasn't long before I decided to move to the west side of LA, where I felt more at home. I found a small rental house in Westwood that would soon be available. "Just watch what these men do when you move to Westwood," Mother Picker said when I told her I was beginning to go out. "Oh, Baby, you're about to learn a lot about men!"

Beginning Again

Six months after Leonard passed, Dorothy Zdenek, invited me to lunch but on our way she told me she had to stop by her brother-in-law's office for an allergy shot.

The doctor invited us into his office after she left the examining room and then the strangest thing happened. Throughout the conversation, he never looked at me. He was pleasant enough, certainly handsome, but I did feel somewhat ignored. His nurse came in and gave him a message. He nodded. "I have a baby to deliver. If it's a quick one, I'll meet you for lunch."

A quick one? This is a new life we're talking about! I was not impressed. All the way to the restaurant, Dorothy talked about her brother-in-law. Oh, she built him up as someone very special. It didn't take long to realize that this was a set up! I wondered if she really needed that allergy shot or if she was just playing matchmaker. In any case, he hadn't seemed interested in me at all. Nor I in him.

We had almost finished a leisurely lunch when he joined us.

"That was a pretty quick delivery," I said, remembering the twenty-two hours I spent in labor with my first-born.

"It was her fourth. It gets easier every time." He made eye contact, but not for long.

"Have you delivered many babies?" I asked. I knew he was a Family Practitioner.

"About a thousand, so far. It's what I like best about medicine."

That stopped me.

When we finished lunch, he asked Dorothy if she and Frank would like to have dinner with him the next night. Then he turned to me. "Can you come with us tomorrow?"

I said I would. He smiled and then something changed. Maybe it was the tone of his voice, maybe it was the tenderness in his gorgeous brown eyes, but I really liked the way he looked at me.

"I'll pick you up about seven." That was his intention, anyway.

The next night it was his brother, Frank, who came to the door.

"Al has an emergency surgery so it may just be the three of us."

Actually, Al arrived just as we were leaving the restaurant, just in time to drive me home. He asked me out again and I said yes. And so it began.

Just before I met Al, I signed the contract to rent a house in Westwood. Shortly before moving day, Frick called and said something like, "I know you're going to be busy with the move, so call me when you get settled and we'll go out to dinner."

Frack called and said something like, "I know you'll have your hands full with the move, so if there's anything I can do to help, please just call me. I'll be right there."

Al didn't even call; he just showed up with moving boxes and packing supplies and pliers to unhook the washing machine. And then while I packed the baby's things, I watched him pick Tamara up from her crib to change her diaper and I remember how he cradled her when she hugged him and surprised us both when she said the word "Daddy" for the first time. And oh, how he pulled Gina into that gentle embrace, when she just stood there looking sad.

On our third date he kissed me and I had an unexpected attack of grief. Al held me when I cried for Leonard. I sobbed and he just kept holding me. I wasn't ready for this. But I didn't pull away. I loved Leonard. But I really wanted Al to kiss me again.

I never had another date with Frick or Frack.

Once I asked Al why he looked away from me on that first meeting. He said he knew that if he looked at me, he would marry me and he was quite happy with his bachelor life. Al was the old-fashioned kind of doctor from Chicago, sort of a Marcus Welby type who not only delivered four thousands babies in his lifetime, but did most of his own surgeries and made house calls long after the AMA advised against it. You'll know how easy he was to love when I share these moments with you:

Years after we married, we were in Ketchikan, Alaska, in a hotel lobby that was packed with people who couldn't get a plane out because of the weather. All the rooms were taken. Al saw a woman across the lobby and with medical intuition based on years of careful observation, he said, "You see that woman over there? She has a migraine. Ask her if she wants to lie down in our room while we're out." She did have a migraine and was grateful for a quiet place to rest.

I loved Al's generosity. He never charged for his services to any housekeeper or gardener in the neighborhood, never a minister, priest or rabbi, never any member of a doctor's family, or anyone else who put their sad story in his ear. One day a nurse in his office told me he was at the hospital delivering a third baby for a woman who hadn't paid for her first. He wouldn't have noticed.

Al was a practical man with innovative thinking skills. When a belly dancer came to his office and needed her gall bladder removed, she was devastated because a scar would put her out of business. Al made the incision under her right breast where it would never show, right over the existing scar for her implant. Her breast covered the gash; the scar would never dance when she moved.

Early in our relationship, Al told me he was never going

to get married again; I think he said that more for his own benefit than for mine. It was a reminder of his intention instead of a declaration. Twice married was enough he said, and both had ended bitterly. I was glad he wasn't looking for a wife because I had no intention of getting married again either.

I really thought I meant that.

It took Al about eight weeks after our first date before he forgot about the delights of bachelorhood and asked me to marry him. I wasn't ready. Loving Leonard and grieving for him still, loving Al and wanting to be with him, scared of being with him, scared of not being with him, I was overwhelmed. If I married Al, I would have two more ex-wives to deal with and four more stepchildren—three of them were teenagers and I was already overwhelmed trying to figure out what was best for my two little girls. I was an only child, raised to act like an adult when I was just a kid—which doesn't provide the best background for that kind of responsibility. The next time he asked me I said it was much too soon. I wasn't ready to think about marriage. But thirteen months after Leonard's death, I became Al's wife.

All the way to the church I prayed, "Please God, if you don't think this is going to work out, just keep him from showing up. It really will be embarrassing if he isn't there, but I'll deal with it."

Leonard had given me a beautiful and unusual engagement ring and I asked Al if I had to put it in the vault. He said, "We're not putting the children in the vault, so why should you put that pretty ring in there?" Instead of an engagement ring, Al put a diamond pendant around my neck. When he slipped our wedding band on my finger, it lay next to the ring Leonard gave me.

It was a small wedding of family and a few friends, in the church I loved. Al and I were married by Louis Evans Jr, who had been Leonard's closest friend. But that is another story.

The honeymoon was—well, it was rather bizarre. After a

perfectly lovely wedding night at the Beverly Hilton Hotel, we went to the airport to catch our plane to Mexico City. It was delayed. After waiting around for hours, we finally went to a hotel near the airport so we could leave early the next morning. Why we decided not to stay in Mexico City after we got there, I simply don't remember. Was it the weather? The crowds? A more interesting option? Whatever the reason, we took another plane to Acapulco, without hotel reservations— we didn't know there were important yacht races going on that weekend. It was impossible to get a room at any of the beautiful beachfront resorts. Then we decided on an unpretentious little hotel, utterly lacking in charm, but at least it was on the beach. We decided to make the best of it. Until we saw the bed.

Al looked as dismayed as I felt. I was always good at hiding disappointment. There were probably bedbugs or fleas or something worse. "I wouldn't mind sleeping on the beach," I said. "I've never done that but I'll bet it's a lot better than sleeping on this bed!"

"Not what I have in mind," he said and as a last resort he called one of his patients who lived in Acapulco and had often invited Al to visit. "He flies to LA once a year for his checkups and every year he tells me to come on down. I never thought I'd take him up on it."

The end of that tale was that we stayed in an enormous house with a private chef and driver, ocean views, beautiful gardens, and total privacy. The gracious hosts rushed to get us settled before their plane took off for California. It was a perfectly wonderful honeymoon.

We settled into married life in a house on the flatlands of Encino. I wouldn't consider living in the mountains and Al understood my fear. He never complained about giving up the city view that he loved when he lived in the nearby hills. We could have been the poster couple for "opposites attract."

Al liked fishing, I liked theater; he liked football, I liked dancing; he read medical journals and science, I read fiction and psychology. I loved discussions about philosophy and art, he liked to drop to the bottom line. On Election Day, we often cancelled each other's votes. But on all the important issues of life, we were a perfect match.

Our marriage was an adventure with the one constant being our devotion to each other. The only things we quarreled about were the temperature of the house, the best wine to serve at dinner parties...and, of course, how to raise children. We certainly didn't always agree, and there were some challenging moments, as there are in every marriage, but neither of us ever said a word that was intended to wound.

Seven weeks after we married, the Picker family was holding a birthday celebration for Leonard's mother at the Plaza Hotel in New York. Al and I were invited and so were the children—as many as we wanted to bring. Al was delighted with the invitation and curious to meet this extraordinary family he had heard so much about. We took Gina, Tamara and Al's youngest son Don, who was just a little older than Gina. The other children were in school. What an amazing time that was. Newly a bride, I was anxious about this meeting, but Al, my brave new husband, seemed totally at ease. The descriptive phrase in the 60's was, "He was comfortable in his skin."

I'm sure the family noticed how my girls adored him, and how gentle he was with them. Before our visit had ended, Mother Picker put a photograph of Al on her dresser and her strong voice sounded tender when she said, "He's my fifth son!"

That was pretty remarkable for a Jewish woman whose "fifth son" was brought up Somewhat-Catholic and her forever-daughter-in-law was a liberal Presbyterian. It seemed just as remarkable that Al accepted this extended family as his own.

Once, when someone mentioned how good Al was to Mother Picker, she said with a perfectly straight face, "Well, it's the least he can do since I put him through medical school!"

Leonard's brothers seemed as close to Al as his own; he gave them advice on medical issues and they told him things about finance. Leonard's youngest brother, Arnold, was especially close to Al. They laughed a lot, avoided discussing politics or religion, and their relationship blended this family into one.

Years later, soon after I returned from visiting Mother Picker in New York, we heard that she was not likely to be with us much longer. She asked to see Al. The next morning, he was on the plane to New York. It was a rare and beautiful love they shared. A true "mitzah" she would have said. Gina went with him, for she needed to say goodbye to her grandmother. Leonard's brother, Eugene, told her she would always be part of this family. I will be forever grateful for how the brothers embraced her when she was so sad.

Ah, the Family

So now we were eight. More than anything, I wanted to give to Al what he was giving to me: a loving embrace to the children we now shared. How I longed for a bucket of wisdom that would help me be the lovable, kind, thoughtful, fair—and ultimately adored stepmother that I imagined would be the outcome of my noble intentions. If you're not laughing now, just wait.

Imagine the guilt I felt when I realized I might never attain that goal. Even if I adjusted my Mission Statement to, "I will not lose my temper, request assistance, or try to change any aspect of the existing code of behavior that was established long before I showed up in their lives."

Al Jr., Gene, and Sherri were wary teenagers who would just as soon their dad hadn't brought this trio of females into their already complicated lives. Don was six, and he wasn't one bit pleased that suddenly a four-year-old Gina and two-year-old Tamara were trying to usurp the lap of *his* daddy. The little girls wouldn't let Al out of their sight when their new siblings were around and they had their own baby-wise, territorial ways of getting his attention. All of those reactions were perfectly normal, of course. So were mine: I was overwhelmed and feeling totally inadequate as I tried to figure out how to bring some form of stability to the little ones while learning how to be a "Sunday mother" for the older kids and a Thursday, Saturday, Sunday mother for Don. And did I mention that I was an only child who grew up in a quiet, orderly house where one did not turn suction-toed frogs loose in the bathroom, keep snakes as pets in the bedroom, or do handstands in the living room?

And Al? Well, he wasn't ruffled by any of this. He loved having a batch of kids and their antics made him laugh. He was totally comfortable with the rising decibels of sound that seemed to me as though the inmates had rioted and insanity ruled.

You can open your arms but if no one runs into them, you need to rethink your strategy. If I cut to the bottom line it was this: To Gina and Tamara, Al was their daddy. To three teenagers and a five year old, he was their daddy *first*. They had their own mothers and had no interest in having an additional one. Who was I and what was I doing messing up their world?

I had a lot to learn. Truth to tell, I wish I had done it better. The reality is that all we can ever do is the best we can. And that I did. Everything from the abundance of books I read on childrearing and the truckload of money I spent on psychologists, psychiatrists and counselors of various persuasions.

Good intentions are not always enough. I thought back over my early years and wondered what I could learn from them. Was I ever a wild and tempestuous teenager? (Hmmmm, we'll get into that.) Sometimes I thought that trying to learn from my own adolescence was like trying to learn Latin from a French cookbook. But as the years passed, the backward journey of remembrance was to prove invaluable in ways I could not have imagined at the time.

I was thirteen when we moved to LA from Dallas and I did not transplant well. I was fiercely homesick. Driven by more compassion than wisdom, my parents let me spend the summer in Dallas. I stayed with one aunt or another, one friend or another and no one ever asked where I was staying or with whom. They had treated me like an adult most of my life and this was no different.

One night there was a slumber party (which, of course means, never-go-to-sleep-until-dawn party). There were five of us and Older Sister, who might have been fifteen. It's beastly hot in Dallas in the summer and in those days, homes were not air-conditioned. It was about two in the morning when we had run out of things to do that we came up with this plan:

We would take the family car and drive to a country club where one of the other girl's parents were members. She knew how we could get in after hours by climbing over the back wall, and we could go into the pool and cool off. "It's really okay," said Sandy, "because my folks always let me bring guests at the club. Older Sister said, "My Dad lets me drive the car sometimes. He won't care." Here's how thirteen-year-old reasoning goes: "The club isn't open and, of course, we wouldn't hurt anything; in fact, no one would even know we had been there! How could that be bad?"

Whatever happened to all that good judgment my parents assigned to me? Or to those well-brought-up-young-ladies who didn't swear or wear inappropriate clothes and went to formal dances with program cards tied on their wrists from the time they were ten years old? Well, let me tell you, all propriety melted away in the heat and we took off driving with Older Sister and a cacophony of giggles.

The grounds of the country club were dark but there was a full moon and, as the song says: *the stars at night are big and bright, deep in the heart of Texas.*

We thought no one was at the club at this hour and yet we whispered in our high soprano voices, and tried not to laugh too loudly, even if everything that was said seemed outrageously funny. And of course, we had no swimsuits.

If I told this story to my daughters, they would say…"So?" But this was 1948 in Highland Park and modesty was required of all young Dallas virgins. I'm sure each of us was fascinated by the opportunity to see if we looked just like everyone else without our prim little panties and training-bras and there was much squealing and sort-of-hiding under the water or behind our towels. Of course the inevitable happened:

We saw a flashlight approaching from the main building. Oh, we were so busted! We all tried to climb up the pool ladder at the same time, bumping and pushing in our struggle for personal safety. We grabbed our clothes and towels and ran toward the stone wall. Now we were all scared to death and someone was crying and five little wet and slippery naked girls must have been a pretty sight trying to escape over the wall in the moonlight.

We made it to the car and took off as fast as bank robbers, fleeing the scene. Everyone was trying to get into her clothes as fast as possible, bumping elbows and yelling '*Ouch!*' Driving naked down Northwest Highway was not at all what we had in mind when we started this adventure.

"Who has my top?" Janie sounded frantic. *"Where is my top!"* Somewhere near the pool, the wall or the street, no doubt, but everyone tried to help and looked under or behind every movable thing or person until we were sure it wasn't there. Remember the heat. No one even started on this escapade wearing more than a halter and shorts. Nothing was left for Janie but to keep a towel over her almost-breasts and figure out how she would explain this loss of clothing to her mother. At this moment, we just wanted to get back to the house as fast as we could.

That's when we saw that a car was close behind us. Too close. We went faster. So did the other car. We turned right. It was only a few feet behind us. Speed was Older Sister's solution but that didn't help at all. And now we were moving further away from town and all of us gave advice at once, none of which was useful.

I had never been in a car moving that fast in all my life. Our lives were in the hands of an inexperienced driver who was scared out of her wits and overcompensated with every turn of the wheel. The car behind us blinked its lights. If it had been a police car, the lights would have been red or there would have been a siren. Surely, a young girl's imagination can really go wild at a time like this. We were all terrified.

Then we were on a country road with no houses on either side and somebody was hysterical, while the rest of us were trying not to be. Then, on the right side of the road, there was a house with a light on inside.

"Pull in there! Somebody's home!"

"Hold on tight," Older Sister yelled and whirled the car off the road and onto a driveway and onto the grass all the way up to the front porch. Our doors flew open and we ran toward the house but the car that was behind us pulled off as well. Then we were all screaming and yelling for someone to let us in.

If people were in that house they were not about to open the door to all the screaming kids. Some of us tried to get back to the car but the boys were standing there waiting for us.

Thank God for the moonlit night. And that I recognized one of the boys. He was on the high school football team and I screamed his name. Everyone stopped like a freeze-frame on film. *"Billy Joe, what do you think you're doing?"* Now I was mad.

When your adrenalin is off the charts and you have enough righteous indignation to create a storm of accusations, even older boys can be taken-a-back. But instead of being humbled, Billie Joe turned into big brother. And he *swore!*

"What the hell do you think you're doing out this time of night!" He smelled like beer and looked like he had plenty of it.

By now the other girls were in the car and I was the last one in as Billy Joe's voice rose and fell while he berated us for our stupid behavior. Then he walked over to the car and in an angry, protective voice he said, "You girls don't even know what could have happened to you tonight! You shape up and go home. *Now!*"

All the way home I kept thinking about what he meant and that's when I was the most afraid.

This memory helped put a perspective on the behavior of teens as I recalled my own adolescent experiences. Wasn't there a time I climbed onto the roof of the Varsity theater just to see if I could? I was so proud of myself for doing that but the problem was that I couldn't get down and someone had to call my dad.

And how about when my soundly-sleeping father was stretched out on his bed taking a nap on a Sunday afternoon in the summertime—my friend Mary Lou and I oh-so-quietly painted his toenails red and then tied them with string to the bedposts?

It's not quite the same thing as letting suction-toed frogs loose in the house or kicking a hole in the dining room door. But remembering my own escapades made me a little more tolerant of the things that went on in a teenage world. A little. But not much.

There was trouble in paradise, that's true, but there was also healing. And eventually peace, love and perspective replaced the chaos of the 60's.

Now that I'm in my seventies, I still don't know what I should or should not have done in those early days. But recently, when most of the family had gathered at the oldest daughter's house, I saw Sherri with her four children, a gaggle of grandchildren, and watched in awe as she herded those adorable kittens without even raising her voice or giving them the demon eyes that warned of an impending storm. I was really impressed with her skills.

Sherri and I have become very close over the years and sometimes we laugh about those hectic days. I remember when Gene gave me my first ski experience by taking me up the chair lift and then showing me how to snowplow on my way down. Sherri remembers that I would put an alarm clock outside the master bedroom door on evenings when she was out. If she came in on time, she just turned off the alarm so we never woke up. If the alarm went off, we woke up and worried until she got home.

Sometimes there was heartbreak in the stories. She remembers the night she came to the front door in tears and barefoot and asked to live with us. Of course, she was welcome and it seemed like a good chance to have a closer relationship. She was a good kid and I didn't realize how much she was hurting. It would have been better if I had listened more and talked less. If I had just been wise enough to be still and let the relationship grow slowly. Sometimes, Sherri and I talk about those times together. Sometimes we ask forgiveness. But always, we end the conversation with a hug.

The Cycle of Life

In the middle of the night, a few years after we were married, Al made deep groaning sounds in his sleep. Frantically, before my conscious mind could even censor the words, I shouted, "Don't you *dare* die!" He woke up as startled as I was, then offered a sleepy smile and pulled me close to him. "Not tonight, I won't die. I promise," he said and went right back to sleep. I was awake for a very long time. I don't know if the term 'post-traumatic stress' existed in the early 60's, but I'm sure 1961 is the year my terrible fear of abandonment and loss began.

The time would come when I would have to face the loss of that lovely man. But not yet.

Al and I were married for forty-five years and one month.

Now, once again, I write the shattering words, "My husband died." With extraordinary courage, he fought diabetes, neuropathy, spinal stenosis, high blood pressure, and a quadruple-heart-bypass. He endured BCG treatments, three cancer surgeries, radiation, and finally, his bladder was removed.

Al went from running up five flights of stairs to the hospital delivery room, to using a cane, then a walker, then a wheelchair, then a hospital bed in our home. Through it all, he rarely complained. He told me every day how much he loved me. Al was the easiest man in the world to take care of.

He wouldn't want me to linger on the details of his illness, though some of it should be told. He would want me to write about dancing in the shadow of grief, about the Spirit that keeps us alive in darkest times. He wanted me to honor my love for him by finding creative ways to live well on this dark path through widowhood. We had talked about such things when we knew the time was near.

Al's story is of courage and of love. After a long fight against the odds and medical predictions, he slipped so gently into the angel's arms.

On the late afternoon of January 13, 2008 Al went to sleep and never woke. He was eighty-six years old. His sense of humor remained with him until the day he passed. If he was reading this over my shoulder right now, he would say "Okay Doll, I wasn't *that* perfect!" But he was.

The year was 1994 when Al was diagnosed with prostate cancer. Then there was surgery. Then radiation. He was doing well for two years. Cancer returned. Surgery again. Radiation again. Weakness was overwhelming. On his seventieth birthday, he retired from his medical practice.

Our home in Woodland Hills, in the suburbs of LA, had many stairs. It didn't seem the wisest place for us to live, after his retirement. In 1998, we discussed putting the house up for sale. We both wanted to move to Santa Barbara, a gem of a community on the beach just an hour to the north of Woodland Hills. Our home wasn't on the market when a broker came by with a client who wanted to buy it with a thirty-day close of escrow. How could we say no? As we were packing, I saw Al climb the spiral staircase to his study and he looked pale. He didn't seem to be breathing normally. Of course he didn't want to "bother the doctor" on Saturday but I insisted. Al didn't care when patients called *him*, of course! He made the call but his complaints sounded so non-threatening, as he described them, it's no wonder the doctor said he would see him on Tuesday. Acting totally out of character, I took the phone and said, "I'm driving my husband to an emergency room. Should it be Northridge Hospital, where Al was a Founder, or Huntington Hospital, where his doctor practices?" Huntington it was.

Al teased me about my sudden burst of assertiveness but wasn't really upset. Especially after the tests were run and then a team of doctors gathered for emergency surgery and performed a quadruple bypass operation on Al's heart on Sunday morning. Not the time one would schedule elective surgery.

I was about half way through packing for the move but now I only wanted to be with Al. I stayed at the hospital and Tamara took over at the house, making all the decisions about what to give away and what to pack for storage. It was a large house with several outbuildings which were full of everything from tennis racquets to party glasses to the kids tennis trophies. Everything Tamara thought I would want to keep would have to go into storage, for I had not had time to find a place for us to live. Some of the kids came to help and Tamara's friend, Judy, flew down from Palo Alto to pack the breakables. At night, Tamara drove to Huntington Hospital and stayed with me on a wing that is provided for worried families.

Al had an easy time with the heart surgery, not at all like the cancer surgeries a few years before. He didn't even need pain medication afterward, which tells you something about his body-mind skills. Or that Tamara is gifted in the healing arts and knows a practice similar to Healing Touch.

I was much too busy worrying about my husband to find a place for us to live. It was strange to realize that when we left the hospital, there would be no home to come home to. The moving van came while we were at the hospital. Everything was taken to storage.

When we left Huntington, we stopped at the escrow office to sign the final papers for the sale of our home. Then we drove to Sherman Oakes to spend a few days with our dear friend, Dr. Mary Christianson. She welcomed us like the family we have become and stayed with Al so I could drive to Santa Barbara to find a place for us to live. Something temporary. Something easy.

On the beach near the Miramar Hotel in Santa Barbara, there are a string of tiny houses. I mean really, *really* tiny houses. But they are right on the sand and the ocean sings to you day and night. It seemed like a great place to heal so I rented a one-bedroom nest for the next three months. As soon as Al was able to travel, we drove to Santa Barbara and settled in to our oceanfront shoe box: taking the next step in the history of our lives.

We had some wonderful years before a physical exam revealed that Al's cancer had returned. It was now in his bladder. There were BCG treatments that were ineffective, then radiation, followed by devastating weakness. One day he handed me the car keys. "Doll, I don't think I should drive anymore. My reactions just aren't what they used to be." The numbness in his legs was the result of spinal stenosis. He never got a ticket; never had an accident. It was his choice to hand over the keys, and the choice was consistent with the way he lived.

My grandfather Earle drove a car when he was ninety-three and no longer able; not even the family could convince him to stop. A mountain accident on a rainy night caused his death and the death of his wife and three innocent people who were simply in the wrong place at the wrong time. I will always admire Al for his decision to stop driving.

Now, he had difficulty hearing, even with his hearing aid. I bought him headphones for the TV, which I swear should be called, "The Marriage Saver" for I'm extremely sound-sensitive and the noise of a television blasting through our tiny house was challenging. His grandchildren called him a Buddha; nothing rattled him. He never lashed out in anger, nor did he ever act like a victim. So often he would say, "Doll, just look how long I've lived!" In January 2007, Al's report showed that he was cancer free. We thanked God and the doctors.

Three months after the news that the cancer was in remission, the phone rang and a voice I didn't recognize called with horrific news: Al's youngest son, Don, had been found dead in a motel in Carpenteria. It was days before his fiftieth birthday. The voice on the phone sounded strange. I didn't even know that what he said was true. Some very destructive people had come into Don's life, drawn to his generosity, taking advantage of his need to be needed, stealing the money he inherited from his mother, taking her jewelry when Don's drinking turned his head away. He fought hard against addiction but he lost the war. We saw it coming but were helpless to change the course of events.

The man on the phone kept talking and I felt numb. I heard myself asking all the questions anyone would ask: What happened? How? When did he die? Where was he now?

Of course, I asked who this stranger was who called, whose voice slurred, who sounded miles from the drama of death and pain of loss.

Finally, the police confirmed the news. The hardest thing I have ever done was to tell Al his son was dead. Denial can hit anyone hard and that was his first reaction. Maybe it wasn't really Don! Maybe there was a mistake. Al was so fragile then and I worried about the shock of this. "Stay here and I'll go down there. We'll know for sure." He looked so vulnerable, grieving while hoping it wasn't true. He wanted to come with me, but I asked him not to. There was no way to know what we would find. It was better if I went alone. On the way down the mountain, I called Tamara and she and her husband, Jeff, hurried to be with Al.

There was no doubt in my mind that the news was true.

We could see it coming: the drinking and the drugs, the yellowed flesh, the distorted thought. No matter how Al tried, there was nothing he could do.

I identified the body. It was Don.

We did what we could to comfort Al, but that was an impossible intention. He was a man who internalized his grief and it seemed to me that all that emotion, pent inside the body of such a fragile man, was putting his own life at risk. Al was not able to see his son one last time. When your child dies, there are no words that comfort.

In September, Al's bladder cancer returned and now it had advanced. I have always thought it was the grief that broke him, damaging his immune system, leaving him vulnerable to the cancer, but I could be wrong.

In November 2007, we went to the Norris Cancer Center in LA, and Al's bladder was removed. A tube was implanted for urine to pass to a bag that was easy to empty. "We can do this," I said. "We'll be traveling in no time." All of his children and grandchildren and great-grandchildren came to be with him and I don't know if they knew they were saying goodbye. I didn't know it then either.

Al did not recover well from the surgery. There were complications. For days after, his hallucinations were terrifying, which is not uncommon for a man his age after a lengthy surgery.

When finally, Al was able to leave for a rehab center, I thought the hard part was behind us but it had just begun. He was unable to progress at the rehab center so they moved him to another place where the demands were less taxing.

Al was depressed in this place. My chosen-brother, Zev Nathan, a dear friend, is a psychiatrist and he loved Al like he was family. One day Zev showed up at the rehab where Al was staying and said he was taking him on a medical leave (he didn't say we were gong to the beach to have lunch on the pier). I think that did Al more good than any physical therapy or medicine they could have given him. Tamara and I kidnapped him again one day and took him to the Chumash Casino where he liked to play the slot machines. He sat in his wheelchair, smiling and laughing. The tube that went from where his bladder used to be to a disposable bag was tucked discretely behind his feet. I began to have hope that he would get better. Al couldn't stay more than a few minutes but for those moments, his spirits lifted and there was a twinkle in his eyes. We took him back to the rehab center. And he gave it another try.

He hated being there. "Take me home," he demanded a week later. It was not a request.

And so we did.

Al had to be repositioned in bed every three hours at night and I wasn't strong enough to do it alone. Jeff Rutherford, Tamara's wonderful husband, stayed right here in the next room, sleeping on a pallet on the floor so he could hear Al, if he woke in the night. Jeff rigged a special water tube so Al could drink whenever he wanted it, sucking through a tube just like cyclists do. The tube hung from the top of our Balinese bed, always at the ready. Jeff bought the newest diabetes kit that made the regular testing less troublesome. If he had been caring for his own father, he couldn't have been more compassionate. Anticipating Al's every need, he listened for any sign of trouble. It was Jeff who heard the frightening sounds of sleep apnea and recorded it so the doctor would know exactly what was happening. Which is why on a certain day, we drove Al to the neurologist who listened to the tape and immediately arranged for more tests.

We were in the car, on our way home, when Al asked me to drive to the beach and down the pier to let him watch the waves, the gathering storm, and the sea gulls, wild and free.

"I don't want to do this anymore," he said quietly and

the words I wanted to say stuck in my throat. Long ago, we made a promise, each to the other, that we would never, we would *never*, beg the other to stay when the time had come. I just closed my eyes and silently prayed for strength. He wiped my tears away and said, "Don't take it so hard, Doll. It's time."

When my grandmother was dying, and the family gathered around her, things did not go well. She said, "I'm ready to go. There are just as many people I love in Heaven as there are here." She was absolutely at peace with slipping out of her body into the presence of her sweet Jesus. But one of her sons begged and pleaded, "Momma, please don't go. Don't leave us, we love you, we need you." She couldn't leave. She pulled back from the light and into her body in the hospital bed where she had a stroke and lived for another seven years, not really here, not really gone, just lingering.

Remembering that, I drove home and did what I had to do. I helped Al into his bed and called Visiting Nurses and Hospice. Our purpose shifted from fighting to save his life to accepting the reality that we had to face. Al wanted to live his final days in our home, peacefully, surrounded by those who loved him so deeply. How gentle and courageous he was, as he prepared for the divine journey, releasing his ties to this world, embracing his future in the hands of a loving God.

Al refused all medicine and asked for chocolate. Tamara said, "No Dad! You can't."

"TZ, if I die with a piece of chocolate in my mouth it will be a good day."

Dr. Berger said, "Give him whatever he wants. Diabetes isn't the priority now."

Then Steve Riley, Tamara's ex-husband, came to give Jeff a break after many long sleepless nights. Just one day before his passing, Al was joking with Steve in what I can only call 'gallows humor.' He was ready to go, but had one more request. Al asked that his dear friend, Lama Tsony, a Tibetan Buddhist monk, come to see him. Tsony lives in France, but when I called, he said he was on his way to New York to address a conference. He would come as soon as his presentation was finished.

Al's children and grandchildren came to be with him, and some great-grandchildren were here too. Donn Moomaw, who was our minister when we lived in LA, drove to Santa Barbara to see him. We were surrounded by love.

The next day, Al said, "Doll, I think I'm going now."

Tamara had always said she wanted to be with him when he passed and she was here, right with him. "I can take you part-way there, Dad, I know how to do that." Her words were confident, but her voice trembled. She talked about those who would meet him, about the freedom of his body and the abundance of love. She caressed his hand as he lay there so peacefully. Zev and his partner Neal Mazer suddenly appeared by the bed. How did they know? We prayed together, cried together, and then Al opened his eyes. "Why am I still here?" he asked, in a surprisingly strong voice.

"I don't know, Sweetheart," I said to him. "We release you, but the timing is between you and God."

He closed his eyes again. "False alarm," he said. Then, a few minutes later: "I guess I'll wait for Lama Tsony."

Tamara and I didn't think Al would be with us until Tsony could get here, so we took a laptop computer and on YouTube, someone had posted a video of Tsony lecturing. Al saw his picture and heard his voice. Al smiled and then slept peacefully.

The next day, in the late afternoon, I was so tired, I lay down on the bed for the first time since the long vigil began, just for a moment to close my eyes; exhaustion pulled me down and I fell asleep.

Some time later, Tamara touched me on the arm and whispered, "Mom..." She didn't need to say more; I heard the truth in her voice. He was only three steps away. I touched his warm body. But he was no longer breathing. I knew he was no longer there.

Again, Zev and Neal appeared; Jeff and Tamara were with me. Someone called hospice. Neal said, "Let's say a prayer." And we did.

It was Jeff who helped me wash Al's body, an act of such finality it broke my heart. Jeff was always there through the long days that led to this moment. I felt so many things at once—a deep relief that Al was free, a terrible sadness that his life in this incarnation was over, a clear realization that he had left his body but that his Spirit would never really leave me.

At his memorial service, we went back to Bel Air Presbyterian Church, where we were married. We made this celebration of Al's life as great a tribute to his philosophy as we could. John West came and offered a reverent and beautiful liturgical dance to The Lord's Prayer. Paul Bergen sang, as powerfully as he did years ago at my first husband's memorial. Gary Demarest offered the Christian message of life eternal before Zev sang from the Jewish tradition, a prayer for those who passed. Lama Tsony arrived in time for the ceremony and chanted a Tibetan Buddhist blessing. Tamara's ex-husband, Steve created a series of photographs of Al with all of his six children projected on a large screen. Cameron, Al's youngest grandson, wrote a poem for Al when he was sixteen and Gary read it at the service:

My Life in the Palm of His Hand

When the light fades into the star-strewn sky,
crossed with the destinies of thousands,
I turn my eyes away from the spectacle which held my future
and played them upon that which held so many people's pasts.
Like the oldest oak in Eden,
Having knowledge beyond comprehension,
sight beyond the eyes,
but sight within the heart.
He feels more than he sees.
He can cure not only the broken bone,

But the shattered heart and dreams as well.
He occupies me in every atom that I am composed of,
every dream I own.
He strives within me for life and hope.
He is my grandfather.

Cameron's middle name is Allen, Al+Len, in memory of both of Gina's fathers.

This was not the typical memorial service but it was perfect for Al. I'm sure it made Al and Leonard smile and the angels hum along with the beauty of it. It may have shocked a few traditionalists who came that day but I stand on this one certainty: Where love is, there God is also.

I refused the ten-gun salute the Army offered at the gravesite. I know how hard it was for Al to endure the sound of it when his friend, General Martin Ostrow, was buried with full honors. And there would be babies and young children who would be terrified by the sound of it. I did accept the flag honoring Al's service as an army Captain and a medic in World War II. Reverend Donn Moomaw offered a prayer and a short message.

I waited to write the wording for the grave markers until Al and his son were there together. For Don, I chose the words I thought he would love most: "Now in his Father's house." For Al: "His loving spirit continues to guide our lives."

It is done.

I believe with all my soul that Al left his body the moment there was no longer a heartbeat, and yet, it was hard for me to separate from that body, that beautiful house he lived in.

I sleep on Al's side of the bed because I cannot bear to wake and see it empty. I do not sit at our dining room table alone. I wrap his robe tightly around me and sit by the fire and comfort myself with memories of our time together. I've learned some things about moving on with life when times are painful. Sometimes I do it well; sometimes I don't. Grief is complicated and hard. At first, there's the sorrow of losing the person you love so deeply. Then there's the adjustment to living in your home alone. And then there is the question that cannot be ignored: *What do I do with my life now!*

Collective wisdom says I should give myself a year without making plans for my future. Take time to heal. Embrace the sadness. Allow the tears. I know the truth in that but also the irony of it. To live without a plan is painful in itself, at least for me. Planning is part of the healing, whether I act on those ideas later, or not. I'm taunted by the old saying, "If you don't know where you're going, any road will take you there."

It's been a long time since I lived alone. 'Living alone' has a different meaning when you're twenty-one, making a movie in Paris, or when you're in the shadow side of seventy, missing your husband, and living in Santa Barbara. In both situations, you have choices to make and—for better or for worse—the show goes on.

You knew it was coming, but suddenly, you're standing at the crossroads without a map and no idea where the roads will lead. Ahead of me, a dozen roads converge at a 'roundabout' and I'll circle many times before choosing the one I want to take. I'll watch the road; I'll look for signs. And I'll keep an eye on my rear view mirror. When you're changing lanes, you'd better know what's coming up behind you.

We cry, we grieve, we move on.

Lost in Paris

Al has been gone for six months and I still feel adrift. I know how fortunate I am to have the options to decide where and how to spend the late afternoon of my life. Gratitude keeps me centered. I am humbled by the blessings that remain, and never take them for granted. But that doesn't prevent the loneliness from overwhelming me, at times.

What do I really want to do now? Where do I want to live?

Much as I love Paris, and it appears frequently as a container for my dreams, would I really want to live in France now, in my seventies, when I am no longer young and feisty? I decide to try it out for a month at Tamara's invitation. She lives in Aix-en-Provence, but I go to Paris first with my granddaughter, Ashleigh. I show her my old apartment building on *Rue de Miromesnil*, where I lived when I was twenty-one. We visit the same places where I went with Al: a small hotel on the Left Bank, dinner at Coupe Chou. We go to a concert at Sainte Chappell, take boat rides on the Seine, enjoy the Louvre, of course, the Eiffel tower, of course, the Musee d'Orsey, of course, which is my favorite because of a certain memory:

Before it was a museum, the Musee d'Orsey was a railway station. In between those times, one end of it became a small hotel. When Al and I had been married for five or six years, we stayed there with Gina and Tamara. I still remember walking to the elevator and peeking over a barrier to see an enormous clock at the far end of the station. The train tracks were still there, looking rather eerie in that dark, lonely space below.

When Ashleigh was a little girl, we took her to Paris. Now we are back again, two women, best of friends, exploring the city I love beyond all others, and one she barely remembers. The weather is perfect; the French are thoughtful and charming, (yes, they are). Paris has changed but not in ways that concern me. It is Paris! I have come here many times over the years but since the day we met, this is the first time I've been here without Al. Everywhere I look, my husband is not there.

I try so hard to pull out of my intensifying depression. This is neither the time nor the place to give in to my sadness and I certainly don't want to ruin this trip for Ashleigh, or for myself. This is Paris! How can I feel this depleted in Paris? No matter how hard I try to pull out, I feel myself slipping into memories that no longer comfort me. I am overwhelmed by everything. I can't remember how to use the metro; I can't remember how to get to places I have been many times. I have trouble working the ATM machine and don't know how much to tip the cabdriver. Anyone who has ever experienced a deep loss, or who knows someone who has grieved, will recognize the common symptoms. I don't even make the connection, which tells you just how abandoned and brittle and lonely I feel. This is Paris! I say to myself. So what? Says my heart.

We take the train to the South of France, where Tamara and Jeff meet us at the station. I try so hard to be cheerful but they clearly see through the attempt. They know me much too well. I see bewilderment in the eyes of my family. Unable to accept that it is I who am bewildered, I'm critical of everyone. Not out loud, of course, but anything I'm thinking usually shows on my face. And they, who love me as deeply as I love them, can find no words to comfort me. All you can do is the best you can do. We are all trying.

It takes me a long time to remember the part that

perception plays in emotions. I consciously focus on gratitude. These are the actual facts: my family is supportive and I had forty-five amazing years with a man I love; I can afford to live in my home; I can travel. *Whatever happens, I'll deal with it.*

So why can't I embrace the blessings and accept the loss? I'm not always kind to myself when struck by an emotion this intense. I feel guilty for my wobbling confidence, angry that I'm not more competent. Of course, it would be wiser to just acknowledge what I feel and sit with the sadness. But as I told you earlier, when it comes to adjusting to life without Al, sometimes I do it well and sometimes I don't. Much as loving people try, no one knows how to comfort at times like this.

Then I remember a moment from the sixties: Our bathtub was the kind that was so popular then—three steps down, double-wide and about seven feet long. If I had relaxed I would have drowned. I was soaking in a lake of sweet-scented bubbles when five-year-old Tamara burst into the room, deep sobs overwhelming her. She was weeping like her heart would break as she immediately stripped all the way down to skin and scampered onto the watery steps, plopping herself down into the warm water, tears streaming down her cheeks.

"Use your words," I said softly as I reached out to comfort her.

And between the hiccupping sound of her sobs, I heard the complaint and understood how deeply her feelings had been hurt. She talked and I listened. And listened. And listened. I rubbed her tiny foot, just to keep contact.

Finally: "Oh, Sweet Pea, I know how much that hurts. When I was your age the same thing happened to me."

Abruptly the crying stopped and her voice was indignant. "Well, just because the same thing happened to you when you were my age doesn't mean that you felt about it then the way I feel now!" And she resumed her wailing at full volume.

It was sweet to realize that my baby girl had that depth of

insight. We think we know how someone feels, but we are only projecting our own experience, imagining that impact on another life. Now, I try to listen without assuming that my interpretation is the same as hers, even when the facts are close to identical. Perhaps Tamara just wanted me to know that this was *her* feeling and had nothing to do with anyone else in all the world. It was *her* emotion, *her* pain. And I had no right to diminish her experience by implying that this moment of sorrow wasn't unique to her.

I thought of that today when someone said to me, "I know just how you feel." Of course she didn't. She just knew that there was a time when life was hard for her and she was sorry that this day is hard for me.

I'm having trouble finding the right word for something important. I hate to say, "My husband died." Not only because it causes a pain so deep it's hard to breathe but because I don't believe that anything except his body died. Not his soul. Not his power. Not his personality. I just know the word 'died' misrepresents what I think and feel about this process of evolving. You may have noticed that I've said he 'passed' but that doesn't feel right either. I think his body died and will stay dead. I think the rest of him is already out of here, continuing in some significant way. I'm not trying to proselytize now, I just want you to know how I feel. His body was just the house he lived in. It was a handsome house, but he doesn't need it anymore.

Some people say things like, "I lost my husband," but that makes me think he might be waiting at the lost and found, or hanging out at some street corner, just hoping you'll remember where you left him. Others say he 'crossed over' which brings to mind a game we played in kindergarten. ("Cross over, cross over, let Janie cross over!") 'He expired' sounds awful. So does 'deceased.' I've even heard people say, 'he left' but that sounds like he just walked out. But saying he passed is really no better. What did he pass? His medical exam? Well, yeah! Or maybe he passed the turnoff on the freeway and needs to double back?

I could go on and on about this, but nothing seems to work for me. If I've mentioned a phrase I don't like and it's one you're comfortable with, please forgive me. I just want to find one word in any language that means the man I love so deeply can't be here with me anymore, not in the physical way that was so lovely when I could touch him and feel the sweetness of him and listen to the kindness in his voice. If it hadn't been the right time for him to escape the circumstances of his life, he never would have left me. So what is the word for that?

I have felt his spirit in my meditative practice many times. But tonight what I really want is the physical husband I love and miss. The one who rubbed my feet while I stretched out on the sofa and read as he watched TV; the one who was my confidant and the best friend I ever had, the one I would give anything to hold in my arms again.

It seems to me that grief has three parts. There is the part that means someone you love has left his body and if that person were in terrible pain, or had a long battle he could no longer bear to fight, you can be grateful he's not suffering. It's all about him, this first part of grief—and the love it requires to release him. I know that even if I had the power to do so, I wouldn't bring Al back to the body he left behind, with all the tubes and pains and hopeless prognosis. I couldn't be that selfish. And even though I can't always stop tears from surfacing when friends mention how they miss him, or when I hear of someone else who faces this same loss and I reach for words I cannot find, I remember how life was for Al and know that it was time.

The second part is about your longing for the special person you love and no one else in the world can heal that wound or tell you how to make the hurting stop. We get through it in our own way, which is different for each of us. I try now to focus on the sweetest times, and let the memories bring me solace. I make peace with the emptiness of my house.

Then there's that third part of grief: *What do I do with my life now?*

That First Step

Next year will be easier. Or so I'm told. This is the season of rollercoaster emotions that range from confidence to despair and rise again to equanimity. One can always long for ecstasy, but that seems as remote as another lifetime.

The only writing I do now is in my journal. That should be enough. But it isn't. Why don't I have a single idea for a new book? Suddenly I'm thinking of my mother. If she were here, she would be saying, "*Stop this, Marilee. You are not the only heartbroken woman in this town!*"

People have many ways of approaching a major decision in their lives. Getting the right idea at the right time makes all the difference. There are experts who can help with this, but I took the advice of Ray Bradbury, author of classic science-fiction books and a dear friend besides. He told me that ideas are like cats. If you chase them they run away, but if you start doing something that interests you, the cats get curious and run back to you. I would like to find the idea that was the right one for me now. I'm getting anxious about my lack of direction. But Ray's idea was good. Just let the cat find you. Most of Ray's work was grounded in childhood dreams and the passion he had for using them in his adult life. I'm in the process of re-living memories so I wonder…what will the cats bring me, if I stop chasing after them so relentlessly?

Things happened in my early life that taught me to cope with the unexpected. Thinking about my younger days has reminded me that I can make a good life for myself, even if it isn't the life I expected. My mother's words come to me now.

"It's okay to do hard things." Now, I consider these words and the challenges I remember and create another mantra for myself: *I can go anywhere I want to go and do anything I want to do, and I can do it alone.*

It is Saturday night and I feel restless. Even a good book doesn't hold my attention. I decide to put on a blue dress that Al loved and go to dinner in a very elegant restaurant. Alone. This is not just a place where Al and I would go to *eat*, but where we would go to *dine*. It isn't that going somewhere alone is new for me. I've traveled alone for years, on book tours and for speaking engagements and going to dinner by myself is no big deal. I've always done that, probably more often than most, but now it feels different to go alone because *I really am alone* and that's what makes it so hard to do. I push back my shyness and walk in. Nothing happens. I have a good dinner. I go home. Why was that so challenging?

Another thing that helps is something really physical. I, who haven't danced for forty years, sign up for five dance classes a week. Jazz, Nia, Rumba, Cha-Cha-Cha, and African dance with drums. After a few sessions of each, I realize this was not a good idea. Great for younger bodies but I keep forgetting, I'm really quite a bit older than I usually think I am.

Then I sign up for a seminar at the Four Seasons Hotel. I don't know anyone there and I'm not even quite sure what the seminar will be about—something about the transmission of thoughts between people. It sounded as interesting as anything else going on in town.

I walk into the garden cocktail party on opening night alone and get a glass of wine alone and then I'm not alone any more. A man comes over and introduces himself and I really enjoy the conversation until I don't like something he says. I move on.

I wander through the garden listening to snatches of conversation. It's an interesting crowd. In a gathering of six, a man is holding court about the premise that energy never dissipates and is absorbed by inanimate objects, particularly in the walls of old buildings; I eavesdrop for a moment but lack the courage to join this cluster of strangers. Another group discusses someone's new puppy and the hazards of 'dog meets fine Persian rug' and I think it's the owner not the dog who needs training but I'm got getting into that conversation. A couple who look very married smile at me and I gratefully respond with a flutter of cocktail party conversation. Tonight, this simple, social event—the kind I've attended for more than half a century—is as challenging as a rite of passage.

I take another glass of wine from the roving waiter. An Embassy party in Paris long years ago slips into memory. It wasn't hard to be by myself then. I clearly remember the evening, meeting interesting people, eating good food, drinking good wine, taking a cab home alone. Not a problem. I start thinking about all those places I went alone. Okay, so I'm not twenty-one, but I still have something going for me. I almost laugh out loud when I think of the line by Judge Judy, "They don't keep me here because I'm gorgeous; they keep me here because I'm smart!"

"Hi," a man says and I realize he thinks I was smiling at him!

Now I laugh out loud and he looks pleased. Bet he thinks it's all about him. He's a nice guy and I settle into proper party mode, learning that he's a psychologist, lives in LA, is up for the weekend, staying at the Four Seasons. It's pleasant, no more, no less. We say goodnight and I leave a half-filled glass of wine on a table. I'm driving.

Moving out the expansive drive, onto the street by the ocean, I turn toward the mountain and around the dark and winding path to my home. I whisper my mantra: "I am safe in my house and I *feel* safe in my house." The key turns in the lock of the front door and my hand searches for a light switch. Next time I'll remember to leave the lights on inside.

*****

The next morning the program starts with breakfast in a conference room of the Four Seasons. I show up early and most of the chairs are empty, only a sprinkling of people at a few of the round tables. I choose to sit alone at a table for eight just to see who shows up. Some very interesting people do. I enjoy talking with a woman who raises miniature donkeys and another is walking out on her billionaire husband who is really very good to her but she wants a different life. I resist the temptation to ask her what kind of life she wants. But of course, she tells me anyway.

At home in my warm bed, I think about the things I've done alone since I was a very little girl. Inviting memories to reinforce successes can be a great source of assurance. Next time it will be a little easier. The confident woman I used to be is now the woman I am becoming.

Just as I'm falling asleep I have a strong sensation that Al is here in the room with me. It is just a comforting feeling. Nothing more.

"How'd I do Sweetheart?" I whisper. Just in case.

In the ninth and tenth month of this difficult time, I would have told you that I am getting through it as well as anyone who loves a man so deeply possibly could. Then it is November and December and I am deluged with memories that weaken me.

It was Thanksgiving morning, November 3rd, so many years ago that Leonard died; November 26 was Al's birthday; my father died on December 7th; Al and I were married on December 11th; then there was Christmas which is always an emotional time. Even the birthdates make me feel lonely. Ashleigh was born on December 5th (but she lives in Arizona) Tamara was born on December 15 and McKenna on Christmas morning (but, at least for now, they are both living in France). My closest friends in Santa Barbara, Zev and Neal, are vacationing in South Africa. Patterns of sadness for my losses are well established at the cellular level, patterns of celebrations for birthdays and anniversaries are broken.

This Christmas, Gina invites me to Arizona; Tamara wants me to come back to France. My stepdaughter Sheri invites me to a huge celebration at her house in Agoura. My wonderful friend, Mary invites me to L.A. So you see, it is my own decision that makes me feel isolated. I just have no will to celebrate. I choose to stay home and try to ignore the significance of dates.

When my ex-son-in-law, Steve, hears that I will be by myself at Christmas, he drives down from San Francisco and stays with me for a week. I tell him I don't want to celebrate Christmas; it's just too hard. I can't even bear to put up a Christmas tree. I do take one string of lights and wrap it around the bronze base of a floor lamp that's shaped like a tree trunk. And I wrap another string around the lampshade, over and over. That's all I am prepared to do this Christmas. We agree not to exchange gifts and to spend the money on some excellent wines.

"What is, is and what isn't, isn't," my Momma used to say, long after the Greek philosopher, Parmenides, argued the truth of it and even before the Beatles claimed the phrase for their own. Of course, it's easier to acknowledge that profound truth in your intellect than in your emotions.

I woke one morning from the turmoil of a dream—in the dream, I was crying and telling a stranger, "My husband died last night." It had actually been fifteen months. I longed for the time when Al and I were together and the broken pieces of me were whole. The day does not begin well.

Today, I could call a friend. I could get dressed and go out. I could use my imagination to pull out of this mood but instead I make coffee and toast and in my nightgown. I watch television. Flipping channels, I see an old friend. He's at the piano, singing, his body moving with the notes. His glasses are dark but his smile is just as bright as I remember.

Stevie Wonder and Al were good friends. He was also a neighbor. We always called him Steve—perhaps to separate the person we cared for from the public personality. I remember the night before Al and I left L.A. for Johns Hopkins Hospital in Baltimore for his first cancer surgery; Steve came to our home with his sister, Renee. It was a sweet and low-key evening. Steve requested that we spend that time together because he cared about Al and wanted to pray for his easy recovery from a difficult surgery. How lovely is that?

I remember when he hugged me good-by and touched the necklace that hung snuggly against my neck. "That's from Africa," he said. And it was. How can a sightless man be so discerning?

Steve's very young nephews often showed up at our door when they lived across the street and would ask me, "Can the man come out and play?" Everyone knew who the man was. And most times, Al would stop what he was doing and go with the boys to hit some tennis balls or they would help him work in the garden, or trim the roses that he loved.

I have two regrets. The first is that it has been so long since I've seen Steve. And the other—well, we were at a party at Steve's house, the only people not of color, and his brother Milton came up to me and said, "Steve wants to see you in the other room."

I went in and he was sitting alone at the synthesizer. "Go on in," Milton said, "He wants you to sit by him on the bench. He's just improvising." Suddenly, I felt shy, which isn't my style. But he played like I had never heard him play before, and the sound of it was classical. It was pure joy. He was improvising, but it made me think of Mozart, though Steve surely would have laughed if I had told him that. I was deeply moved, not only by the power of his music, but because he chose to share it with me. I will never forget that night.

Nor will I forget that when I sat there—I have no idea how long—at some point I heard my husband walk in the room and say, "Doll, I have to take out a gall bladder at 7:30 in the morning and we have to go. " 'Night Steve! It was a great party."

Why did Al have to do that!

And of course, the real question is, why didn't I just say, "You go on. I'll walk home later." We lived just across the street.

I have a few regrets in my life, though not many. That's one of them. May Gloria Steinem forgive me; old habits die hard.

The year was 1995 when I answered the doorbell to find Steve's sister, Renee, standing there with a man I didn't know. Renee said she wanted to show her friend our house—she heard we were planning to sell. I liked him right away. He was a tall, handsome man with a rich speaking voice and a quiet demeanor. Her friend's name was Jermaine Jackson, which meant nothing at all to me. Since I didn't actually live in a submarine, I suppose I should have made a connection to his brother Michael, but the at that moment, his name meant nothing at all to me. Of course, I knew about the Jackson Five, but Jermaine was off my radar.

After a brief tour of the house, we sat in the living room making small talk. When there was a lull in the conversation, I turned to him and said, "So, are you in the music business too?"

I don't know how they kept from laughing, but neither cracked a smile and in his lovely, soft voice, Jermaine Jackson said, "Well, I try."

Much later, when my children told me who Jermaine was (and after I recovered from the embarrassment) it occurred to me that it's really okay to make a fool of yourself every once in a while. It's humbling, that's for sure. And the best part is, when you can laugh at yourself, it takes the sting out of the memory.

Fathers and Daughters

How many ways can you stimulate memories of the seasons of your life? Music, of course. Or a taste that reminds you of a person or a place. (Remember Proust and the madeleine from *Remembrance of Things Past*?) The scent of a certain aftershave (How many years since you thought of the man who wore that?) And then there are the photos and the letters.

I open the boxes that hold Gina's memorabilia from the day she was born. On every flat surface in my office, they are sprawled in some semblance of order. My desk holds the photos and collectables of the early days: her first-father holding her like she's the most exquisite baby in all the world; her second father looking at her with such adoration. Birth announcement, grade school report cards, letters from camp, pictures from every stage of her life. Here's one with a cluster of books around her that remind me of how well she read before she started school and oh, how she loved a good story. On the conference table I place the middle grade adventures, the photos of our family travels to Tahiti and Hawaii, Mexico and Canada. High school photos are on different sofa pillows for different ages. (It's challenging for right-brain people to be linear but I'm working on it.) I collect the tokens of her passages as I make a photo album of her life story from the first photo when she was born, until she left for college. She has a birthday coming up and when I started this project, I didn't realize how emotional it would be for me to make this gift for her.

Oh, there's her high school sweetheart, Ralph Davis! Just look at that gorgeous boy. I pluck the sweetest stories of her young life from the hundreds of possibilities and wonder if she will relive those moments and recognize how they shaped her life. I hope I'm choosing the right ones.

Music is a time machine that can take you back to a specific memory of place or person or feeling. If I heard *Stella by Starlight* or *Body and Soul*, I would instantly think of a certain boy named Bob who played those songs on the piano when I was thirteen while I stood there listening, falling deeply into puppy love.

I'm in Phoenix, visiting my daughter, Gina, and the car radio plays the song, *I Wish I Could Dance With My Father Again.* She pulls off to the side of the road and covers her eyes. Gina can't stop her tears, nor can I. We are crying for Al, but also, at a cellular level, for Leonard, for my father, my mother...each loss builds on the sorrow of the loss that came before.

When Gina was a little girl, I held her when she cried for her first daddy and nothing I said or did could make it better. I feel just as helpless now. Perhaps the only thing we can do for each other is just to be present and let the feelings take their time. I ache for Gina in her sorrow, for the loss of her fathers and for my own.

Later when I'm lying in bed, I think about that song and those times in Dallas when I was a child, when we danced in our living room—my mother, my father and I. My daddy would lift me with his right arm, and I would hold onto him by reaching around his shoulder. Momma was part of the embrace as the three of us moved to the music. I remember how my father twirled me around, just like the song said.

He was fifty-two when he was building a house for Leonard and me in Squaw Valley, giving directions on the job site when suddenly, mid-sentence, his heart stopped beating and he was gone. Gina had cried for him then too, tiny girl that she was. His passing was her first loss.

I wasn't the only one who thought my dad was bigger than life. He had a strong, quiet way about him that people trusted. He told the truth and told it straight. And he stayed calm no matter what was going on.

When I was a student at Santa Monica High School, I gave only one party, but that night dozens of motorcycles roared onto the lawn to crash the event. My father told everyone to lock all the doors and turn the lights out. And be silent. We were.

"Shouldn't we call the cops, Mr. Earle?" someone asked.

"No need for that. I'll just go outside and we'll talk a while. You keep this door closed, now. Don't open it! You hear me?"

"Yes, sir," I said.

He went into the front yard, stood before them like the Texas Rangers always did. I listened, my ear to the door. "Now boys, I want you to know that each and every one of you is welcome in my home. You can come back and visit my daughter, but only one at a time." He said more that I don't remember. Then I heard their motorcycles rev and they moved on. When they were gone, one lingering boy said, "Mr. Earle, you're really something. We would have wrecked your house if we'd come in!"

His calm voice didn't change in volume or tone: "I'm mighty glad you decided not to. We're much obliged." (That was a very Texas phrase.) "Come back and see us some other time, young man."

Fortunately, the boys forgot about me and never showed up after that. How many fathers could have pulled that off in those days? My daddy, that's who. An amazing man.

When we were still in Dallas, and he was principal of Armstrong Elementary School, there was something he did on occasion that really won the admiration of the students. After the school day ended, he would take off his wool coat, tuck his tie in his shirt, and do a handstand in the hallway. Then he would walk down an entire flight of stairs on those large, strong hands, his big feet reaching for the ceiling, steady as he went, with coins falling out of his pants pockets. He always let the students take the money home with them.

On occasion, he climbed trees to liberate children whose adventurous natures exceeded their ability to complete their exit strategies. I confess that I was one of them. People trusted him and he ruled like the most benevolent dictator. I was so proud of him.

One day he came into my room at school and said that we would be having a new student in our class. He talked about the interesting last name she had and thought it would be good for all of us to know how to spell it before she arrived. This would make her feel more at welcome.

My school was full of names like Smith and Jackson and Monroe, and other names that came to this country from England in the early days. The new student's last name was Szilagyi. Some students laughed, but most of us were fascinated; it was not in our frame of reference that such a name existed. But before Monday morning came, my dad insisted that everyone in that class could spell her name, S-z-i-l-a-g-y-i and we couldn't wait to meet her. She had star status before she even walked through the door.

My father didn't say he loved me very often, but he frequently said he was proud of me, and I thought it was the same thing. He was always fair. I never heard him raise his voice in anger.

I remember this story only vaguely, but I heard it told so many times that it is implanted in my recollections of childhood, one step removed from my own experience. When I was three and we still lived in Menard, I walked with my father on a path made by car tracks in West Texas. Running ahead of him, I reached for a rattlesnake that was coiled beside the path, probably I was enchanted by the sound and the beauty of its pattern. My father shot the rattler before it could strike.

In those days, he always carried a gun. His life had been

threatened by some renegade preacher who was upset when Daddy sent his daughter home from school because she had the mumps. The preacher said he was a holy man and his daughter couldn't be sick. My father did not give in and refused to let her return to school and the threats started. My father never drove the car in a dark garage the whole time we lived in Menard. His gun was in a holster at his hip, just in case.

On the day he shot the snake, Daddy cut the rattle off and gave it to me as a toy. I took it home and just for fun, I shook it behind my mother who was washing dishes. She whirled around, knife in hand, ready to kill until she saw that I was the one making that dreaded sound.

It was a most challenging day.

What do I really remember about my father and how he shaped the woman I became and am becoming?

There's one incident I will never forget, though I was a very little girl when it happened in Dallas. I came home from kindergarten singing a song I had learned with a very catchy melody. The words had no meaning for me, certainly not the double entendre nor the less-than-subtle anti-Semitism. My father's voice was cold and quiet. He put me in the car and we drove miles across Dallas while I was trying to figure out why I was in so much trouble. He took me into a small shop. A man with a big smile and a long white beard, just like the pictures of God in our Bible, came to greet us. I had never seen a beard in real life, nor heard a man speak with a foreign accent.

My father picked me up and sat me on the counter; the memory of cold glass on my bottom remains 'til this day. None of their words stuck in my memory. The man with the long white beard was trying to be very nice to me I could tell, and he had something in his hand. It was for me. It looked like a cracker and I said thank you, before I put it to my mouth. He had beautiful brown eyes and a funny way of speaking and I wondered if maybe he was God, after all. On the way home my father talked a lot more than he usually did and he must have had plenty to say about the respect one should have for all people. The only thing I took from this lesson was that I should never sing naughty songs and Jesus was a Jew and liked matza and Jews were very special people and God was a very nice man.

After Leonard and I married, we were at a nightclub where the entertainer was telling terribly rude jokes about Jews. Why was Leonard laughing! This was not a good thing! Suddenly, I felt like the little girl sitting on the remembered glass counter and my father saying things I did not understand. I wanted to leave and vividly remembered the dry non-taste of matza. It was all very confusing and my embarrassment was painful. Some lessons you never forget.

Dallas was a conservative town and my parents were liberal thinkers. My Aunt Winifred didn't speak to anyone in my family for a year because my dad voted for Roosevelt. Conservative values and great pride of heritage were in the core of her spine and she took enormous pleasure in telling stories of deeds done before either of us were born. My father had a different relationship with the past. He said, "You make your own reputation and leave the dead alone."

My dad would praise achievement, but never appearances. I do recall him saying I looked pretty or "mighty fine" when I was all dressed up. But never more than that. He believed it was appropriate to feel proud of what you worked hard to achieve, but never something as superficial as how you looked. After all, you didn't do anything to earn your looks so it should never be a point of pride. If someone said I was pretty, it meant no more than if they said I wore a pretty necklace. It was like saying the sky is blue; the day is cold. The world is full of pretty faces.

Other fathers would say, "Have fun" or "Be good" when my friends left home. My dad would say to me, "Use good judgment." That required constant assessment of the situation.

Were they too strict or too permissive? The definition of good parenting skills changes with every generation.

When I had my babies, I didn't want to raise them the way I was raised. What was so wrong with the way they brought me up? I was trusted implicitly. I was loved. But I blamed the severe migraine headaches I had from the age of four, on the high expectations and the fact that I wasn't ever allowed to "talk back," sulk, whine or ask a second time for anything if the first answer was 'no.'

Because I climbed on everything from his shoulders to tree branches to jungle bars, one of my father's favorite nicknames for me was Monkey. My best friend's daddy called her Princess and I was jealous of the title. I told him so, and he said, "I'm not raising you to be some silly princess! You are more valuable than that."

I was expected to be brave. When I saw the movie "Wolf Man," at a Saturday matinee, I was convinced there was a real man who could turn into a vicious killer and that he was probably hiding in one bush or another, waiting for the full moon.

My father stood with me at the front door of our house early in the evening the night I saw that film. He insisted I run around the house by myself and he would wait for me. He said I would be safe and this would help me get over my fear. I did what he said but I'm sure he didn't know how terrified I really was. I hated the dark. At night I would stay awake wondering if something in the closet would get me if the alligators under my bed didn't snatch me first. I don't doubt that he thought his actions were the best way to deal with my anxieties. His heart was kind, but his obsession with bravery was hard to live up to.

When I was little, my parents never left me with a baby-sitter. When they went to a friend's house for dinner, I had my dinner at home, then went with them to their party and was put to bed upstairs, sometimes under an array of winter coats, both wool and fur. It was not a good feeling to be left in so many different places but I could usually hear their voices and their laughter drifting up the stairs. Sometimes, I didn't feel lonely at all.

I probably misbehaved as much as any other kid, but I was never punished for making a mistake. However, if I sulked or pouted, whined or begged, that was not acceptable and my father's playful eyes would turn stern. Point taken.

The harshest thing he ever said to me was, "Boots! You are acting like a child!" I was nine. Maybe ten. There were some strong expectations in my family but there was as abundance of love and respect for creativity and individuality. It was a rare philosophy for the 1930's and 40's. I know how lucky I was.

My birth name was Mary Lee Earle. I changed it to Marilee when I was thirteen and we moved to California where people insisted on calling me Mary. I'm not a Mary. But in my little girl years, everyone, including my teachers at school, called me Boots. There are three possibilities as to why.

1.) There was a comic strip that was quite popular then and Boots was the name of the protagonist. And like all mothers of that era, mine wanted me to be pretty and popular.

2.) I was given a pair of white cowgirl boots when I was three years old and I wore them everywhere.

3.) I have big feet.

Guess which one I think is the real reason.

Checking the Rearview Mirror

Back in 1944, there were no televisions, no computers, no iPhones, no video games, and maybe not a lot of discretionary income but I didn't notice that. After all, we had lightning and thunder and occasionally hail. We had time to think and dream. We would drive outside the city and just listen to the crashing thunder and watch the storm, or talk about my favorite subject. Me.

Sounds exciting, right?

In one of those long rides in the rain, a ten-year-old girl with stringy hair, legs too long, feet too big and freckles on her nose, who never was a straight 'A' student, leans forward from the back seat and says: "I'm almost finished writing my book, will you check my spelling?"

"Of course. Then you can write your next one." My mother said I was supposed to write important things, or why would God have made me so ambitious? I don't think she had even an inkling about the part she played in my obsession.

From the time I was a child, I was determined to be a writer. At sixteen, I already had a box full of rejection slips and collecting them had stopped being fun. By the time I was fifteen, no one had published a single short story and my novel hadn't found a home, either. It seemed much easier to be an actress. I had good parts in several Equity theater productions and the lead in school plays. It seemed logical to take the easy route and become an actress while I honed my writing skills. (Really?)

I graduated high school a week after my seventeen birthday and enrolled at UCLA as a Theater Arts major. The day came when I had a history final at the same time I was to read for a part at Paramount Studios and the talent scout who asked me to be there couldn't (or wouldn't) reschedule. Now let's see: is this a hard choice? We have a final exam on one hand and the possibility of starting a movie career on the other. Guess which I chose?

The day of my audition, I walked into the studio with stars in my eyes and a head full of unreasonable expectations. In my imagination, first I would be a contract player and then quickly rise to stardom. I knew I would give a powerful performance and a contract would be right there for me to sign.

So much for magical thinking. It was a long fall from the height of my fantasy to the floor of reality. Either the director didn't like my face or my acting or maybe both but in any case, the answer was no.

Adolescent reasoning assessed the problem and came to a clear conviction: if I was ever to be a success, I had to get out of UCLA and devote myself to what I brazenly called my "career."

Although they rarely tried to influence my choices, there was wailing and gnashing of teeth from my family and they reminded me that even my grandmother had a college degree from the University of Texas, and on my father's side, Cousin Hallie Earle actually got her MD degree from the University of Texas Medical School—and that was in 1907! I listened politely but held strong. I could always get my degree, I told them. (And I did—*many* years later.) I argued that my youth would fade and no one would hire me as an actress if I waited until I was twenty, the age I would be when I graduated if I stayed at UCLA. "You have to make it when you're *young!*" I told them. Oh, I was so full of it.

To prove to them that I was serious, I called Charles Meeker, who managed the State Fair Musicals in Dallas, and asked him for a job that summer. He took the call because in those days an operator said, "Los Angeles is calling" and who knew—I might have been someone important. He was very kind and said he would call if he had a spot for me. I really hated that kind of answer.

I asked my parents for the money to go to Dallas. I had none of my own because my father wouldn't allow me to work—he said I could have a career but not a job. That still makes no sense to me. In any case, he gave me the money and this time I took the plane.

I showed up in the office of the director of the State Fair Musicals without an appointment. It was a rather large theater, seating over 4,000 people. Somehow I talked my way in past the secretary. "I'm here, Mr. Meeker," I said and plopped myself down in the chair across from him. We chatted for a moment.

"Do you sing?" he asked.

"No."

"You're a dancer?"

"Not really."

"So what exactly do you do?"

"I'm an actress!" I said, beaming at him.

"But these are musicals," he said quietly.

He gave me the job anyway and the director George Schaefer created a little walk-on part for me in the musical *Carousel*. No lines. Just a chance to get my feet wet in with the troops. In hindsight, I can only say that they were both amazingly kind men. I had no business being there. When we started rehearsals, I was supposed to flit around on stage with some invented busywork. Then the lead actor came on stage—he was from the Broadway show—and oh, my goodness was he gorgeous. I was supposed to flirt with him but instead when he opened his arms to the audience at the end of his first song, I flew into them. Just felt like it. Did it. George Schaefer liked what I did and kept it in the show. He also gave me the part of Joan Blondell's secretary in *Call Me*

Madam, which started rehearsals even while *Carousel* was still running. It was a real speaking part, just like I wanted.

On opening night, with a stage full of Broadway pros, I picked up the phone and said my first line: "Mrs. Adams, you're wanted on the phone."

But no Mrs. Adams walked on stage.

So I said it again. Still, no Mrs. Adams.

Do you think any one of those pros would help me out? No. I had to ad-lib for myself while they just looked amused. I have no idea now what I said, but it got a laugh and I liked that. I said another line and they laughed again. All four-thousand-plus of them. Then Mrs. Adams sashayed in as if she hadn't screwed up her entrance and I said my exit line and left the stage. I went straight for the bathroom, where I promptly threw up.

When I was nineteen, almost twenty, we were having a family vacation at the Sands Hotel in Las Vegas. I was getting out of the pool and a man came up to me who said he was Jack Entratter, the Entertainment Director of the Sands. He asked me to join the show. Would I like to be in the chorus? We were talking when Jerry Lewis came up; he ignored me completely, and started talking with Mr. Entratter.

"Excuse me," I said to Jerry Lewis with a slight tilt of my sassy little chin, "We were having a conversation." While he was deciding what to say to that, I turned to Jack Entratter and thanked him for asking me to join the show, but I said I was an actress, not a showgirl.

I thought that was the end of it. He knew my name and it could not have been difficult for him to find out where I lived, after all, my parents were listed in the phone book. Everyone had a listed phone number in those days. (At least the kind of people I knew.) After I got back to LA, there was a call from Mr. Entratter's secretary. He would like to see me in his Beverly Hills office. Should he send a car?

I stumbled on that one. Someone would actually send a car for me? I said I would meet with him, but I would drive myself.

My mother was frantic. Over-the-top frantic. Afraid for me to go, and even more afraid that my refusal to go would upset a gangster. She thought everyone in the Las Vegas hotel and casino business was with the Mafia.

"Mother, he's a very nice man and I'm sure he's not with the Mafia!"

"You don't know that!" Oh, she was worried. So she went along with me and said she would wait in the car while I had my appointment. I'm not sure what she thought would happen or what she could do about it anyway, but she wanted no part of any of this for me. "You're an *actress*," she reminded me. "Not a showgirl." My thoughts exactly.

So I left her in the car and went to the meeting.

"Come on," Jack Entratter said. "I really want you to join the show. Let's see what we can work out." Such a nice smile. I was sure he wasn't a gangster.

"I won't go to Vegas unless you build the show around me," I said, thinking that would end the conversation.

And here came those words again: "Do you sing?"

I did not.

"Do you dance."

Not very well.

"So you're an actress. I see. What have you done?"

"Well..." This was not going the way I expected. "I have my own radio show on KFVD and I tell Bible stories to children."

"I'll get back to you," he said as the meeting abruptly ended. I never heard from Jack Entrater again.

My mother was overjoyed to see me and couldn't have been happier about the results of the meeting. Actually, Jack Entrater had a reputation of being a kind and gracious man and her accusations were based solely on her stereotypical thinking.

*****

When I was a child, my parents always wanted me to be self-reliant and to believe that I could do anything in the world I wanted to do. They raised me to believe that no matter what happened, I could always take care of myself— and they made sure I had a great deal of practice.

I was about nine, maybe ten, when I got braces, a procedure that required many trips from Highland Park, in the suburbs of Dallas to downtown. My father told me I was old enough to go by myself. He showed me where to catch the bus and what the sign on the front of it would say. He told me the place where I was to get off downtown and he said I could just walk across the street and up a few blocks to the dentist's office and take the elevator to the fourth floor and turn left. "You'll remember Dr. Bowman's office," he said.

I remember being scared about that but trying not to let on. It was years before I learned that the first time I went by myself, my father followed the bus in his car all the way to downtown Dallas, just to be sure I really knew where to go.

On one visit to town, he told me to go to a certain department store and buy a new pair of shoes. At the time, I had never shopped alone but he said it was time I learned and gave me some money. I didn't know for many years that he called the store before I arrived, spoke with a saleswoman and asked her to watch out for me. He wanted her to be sure I bought proper shoes for school and to not let me get something too small; he knew I would want the smallest size I could fit into because I was self-conscious about my big feet. The saleswoman was very kind and I remember feeling extremely capable because none of my friends had ever gone alone to downtown Dallas, and certainly not to buy a pair of shoes without their mother's help. I think the shoes were brown and ugly but I'm not sure I thought that at the time. I do remember feeling very grown up.

After I bought the shoes, I went to a coffee shop and sat at the counter. The waitress asked what I wanted. I told her to wait while I counted my dimes and nickels on the counter; I had to be sure there was enough to pay for a hamburger and still have money for the bus ride home. There was. When it was time to pay the check, the waitress said, "Don't you worry, honey. A man who was sitting at the end of the counter paid for your hamburger." I looked up but the man was gone. I will always remember the kindness of that stranger I never met.

One Christmas, when I was eleven, my Aunt Winifred gave me a season ticket to the Dallas Symphony. The programs were at night and my parents would drop me off at the front of the theater and pick me up there after it was over. I sat in the balcony on the first row. My aunt and uncle had tickets in the orchestra section and one time when they had other plans, I got to sit in my aunt's seat, up front. An elderly woman sat next to me and we talked during intermission. We liked each other a lot; the next time there was a symphony, that sweet old woman gave my aunt a wrapped gift and asked her to deliver it to me. It was a delicate twenty-two karat gold bracelet made of yellow, white and pink gold. It was so delicate it broke on more than one occasion. I kept it until it burned in the Bel Air fire.

I loved music and once when I was ten or eleven, I took a bus by myself on a Saturday morning to the other side of Dallas to hear my first opera. It was *Faust*. I liked it even more than I liked 'Country Western.' I was hooked. My mother said she only liked music she could dance to. My father was tone deaf. I always went alone.

Doing things by myself started early. I mean ridiculously early. My father's brother, George, and his wife Ella, moved to an apartment in Highland Park. I wasn't old enough to start school but they invited me to spend the night with them. I didn't know these people my parents trusted and recall feeling anxious. The next morning, I woke up early and hungry. They were asleep and of course, I didn't want to wake them. Being very quiet, I got dressed and walked out the front door and down the street because I knew there was a store on the corner that had a counter and I had seen doughnuts in the window. Climbing up on a bar stool, I placed my order. I don't remember what I ordered but odds are that it was hot chocolate and doughnuts.

Did I have money with me? At age four? Probably not. As things turned out, I didn't even need it.

Apparently, my uncle woke up and discovered that I was gone. He panicked and called my parents. You can just imagine what they were thinking. My father must have known me well enough to anticipate what I would do because I remember being surprised to look up and see him walk through the door of the coffee shop. I don't know if they had already called the police or not. I just know I never spent the night with my aunt and uncle again. It was probably *their* decision.

I didn't see much of my mother during World War II. She had two brothers who were serving overseas in the Air Force and in the spirit of patriotism and family support, she set out to join the war effort. She was a whiz at math and extremely imaginative but her brains were generally not the first thing men noticed about her. Even so, the boss of the engineering department at Southern Aircraft gave her the job. He had once been her student when he was in school and it was her good fortune to be hired. So my mother designed the jigs that built warplanes. (I think she worked on the B29 but it might have been a B some-other-number.) Seeing her leave for work before dawn, or coming home long after the sun had set, it was hard to remember how she looked in her real life with her beautiful dresses and drop-dead-charming manner. She was once a debutante and was even crowned 'Duchess of the Cotton Palace,' which was a big deal in Texas in those days. Now she wore heavy wool pants and flat-heeled shoes and took a small heater to the plant because the Quonset hut where she worked was bitterly cold in winter. I'm sure it contributed to the arthritis that pained her so badly in later years. Sometimes I washed her silk stockings at night because she always looked so tired. I missed the way my mother was before the war. But my grandmother said we all had to give up something to keep the country safe and I should be grateful that my mother knew how to build airplanes. And I should remember that my best friend had a daddy who was a marine and fighting in France. At least I knew my mother was safe.

When she was a girl, her name was Perla Dickason, which has a lovely cadence when you say it. But when she married my father, she became Perla Earle (the last 'e' is silent) and if you say it aloud right now you'll realize that she must have loved my father very much to be stuck with the sound of P-e-r-l-a E-a-r-l-e, which does not trip easily off the tongue. I thought she could at least have changed her first name to create a better cadence.

Before the war, she used to dance a wild Charleston and always looked so beautiful and feminine, you might not have noticed that she had an analytical mind and was a whiz at engineering. The war set women like my mother free from the assigned role of *housewife*. She, and others like her, paved the way for me to be an international speaker, and Gina to sell real estate and Tamara to design and build beautiful houses, and my granddaughters to be anything they wanted to be so long as there were willing to work for it. I hope they will never be told that familiar phrase: "Now why would a pretty little girl like you want to do a job like that?"

My father's name was John Baylis Earle but he was known as Baylis or J.B. He tried to enlist in the Air Force, but he was considered too valuable on the homefront so they wouldn't take him. In those days, he was principal of Armstrong School, which was a very fine school in Highland Park. One year, the highest-ranking graduates from West

Point Academy and from Annapolis had graduated from that small school that he ran in the suburbs of Dallas.

Dad was on his way to being a doctor when my parents married but he lost his funding when the depression hit and he had to find work. He now had a bride to support. He did what he had to do and became a school principal in the small town in Menard, Texas (which is really in the boondocks) and later in Highland Park (which is very spiffy.) When we moved to California, he became a building contractor, but that's another story.

We moved to Los Angeles when I was thirteen, to follow my father's dream. He always loved to build things and most of all he wanted to build houses. My uncle, Jim Dickason, was a building contractor in Beverly Hills and built some of those grand mansions that had elevators and exquisite woods and elegant details. He invited my dad to join him in business. Hence the move.

My uncle's life was not as settled as it seemed. It was only a few years before the front page of the Los Angeles Times ran the headline: "Ex-millionaire commits suicide over gambling debt." The family was devastated. And ashamed. In addition to grieving the loss of her half-brother, there was the stunning reality that this delightful man had a secret life and no one had seen this coming.

After Jim Dickason's death, my dad was on his own. He started his own construction company and built many beautiful homes in the LA area and in Tahoe. Mom, ever the creative force in our family, designed the houses and drew the floor plans. His company did well and he had followed his dream of building homes, after his plans for being a doctor fell with the stock market crash in '29 and the pleasure he took in being a school principal had run its course. He was a fine and happy man who died at fifty-two. I was still grieving the loss of my father when Leonard died.

*****

When we moved to L.A., I did not transplant well. Thirteen isn't an easy age for any girl to move away from friends but I was optimistic at first. As we drove west, I had daydreams about how wonderful my life would be—I would meet movie stars and go to the beach with new friends. I would try to forget about the boy who was nineteen and went to SMU and how much I was in love with him. Some people thought he was too old for me. Imagine that. I would write stories about my love and my adventures. My dad assured me that I could go back to Dallas for visits; maybe my friends would come to stay with me next summer.

Housing was tough in LA in the late 40's but we took what we could get. The house itself was fine but the neighborhood made my mother nervous. You do what you need to do and my dad said we would find another place soon. When September came, it was exciting to start a new school, but scary, too. Actually, it was pretty traumatic. I was different. 'Different' is not a complimentary word in the teen years. That first day at lunchtime, I saw a group of girls who looked really nice and I went over to them, just like I was taught to do at home in Dallas. I smiled my sweetest smile, extended my hand, and said, "I'm Marilee Earle." They just stared at me. My hand fell to my side and someone giggled. That could be the snapshot for all my school experiences in California. I just didn't fit in or know how to do it.

School in LA was very different from my school in Dallas. In Highland Park, you had to say yes ma'am and no sir, raise your hand before speaking in class, and never *ever* sass a teacher. Sometimes there were dances for cotillion and even at my age we wore formal gowns and had programs tied on our wrists where boys would write their names, claiming specific dances with the girl of their choice.

In LA, there was a lot of swearing and rowdy classes and boys with pants nearly falling off their hips and girls who dressed in ways for which my father surely would have sent them home. And here in LA, after gym class, you were required to strip naked and run through a trough of showers holding your towel high above the spray so it wouldn't get wet.

That's not the way it was done in Dallas. One day as I came out of the spray, a girl came up to me and whispered, "They're going to beat you up after school." I didn't know what I'd done to make them say that. And I didn't know what to do. Surely, it must have just been some kind of weird joke. Then, in my next class, the teacher told me to go to the principal's office. What had I done!

Nothing. Nothing except be different in a place where different wasn't cool. Only in those days, cool only referred to the weather. The principal told me that I would be excused from my last period and should go straight home. He said there was a rumor that some girls were planning to beat me up and he wanted me to be on my way when they got out of class.

Remember how my parents taught me that I could always take care of myself? Well, in this case my father made an exception. He made an appointment with the superintendent of schools and demanded that I be transferred to another junior high.

The superintendent refused. He said I must have said or done something to offend them but I didn't know what I could have done wrong; I had tried so hard to be their friend. The man then said I was spoiled. You have no idea how angry this made my father. If there was one thing he made sure of, it was that I was not spoiled. When my dad was angry his voice got very quiet, even deeper than deep and his eyes looked even greener than they were and he spoke only a few words but they were always powerful and explicit. I can hear the sound of his voice when I close my eyes to remember but I don't know what the words were. It's probably just as well.

I just know that I didn't go back to school until my

parents found an apartment in another school district. I was enrolled at Emerson Jr. High and started over again. I had learned not to shake hands with girls my age but thirteen years of strict behavioral attitudes are hard to break. No one tried to beat me up at Emerson, but I can promise you I never made Homecoming Queen. If they even had such a thing.

I cried myself to sleep many nights, skipped classes with my mother's permission, kept my grades up and even wrote a play that the drama department presented to the school. It was about a girl whose fiancé went off to fight the Germans in World War II. The teacher asked my mother how I could possibly have written that play; how could a thirteen-year-old girl understand those feelings of love and loss?

She didn't know how much my love for a certain boy had deepened since we were separated. I think my parents took quite a chance sending me back at Christmas for the holidays. Nothing happened physically, but emotionally, I was as in love as any fourteen-year-old girl can be.

The next summer I was still missing that lovely boy but they said I couldn't have a plane ticket for Dallas, and if I wanted to go, it had to be on the bus.

Did they really think I would refuse to ride a bus for sixteen hundred miles in the summer heat before buses were air-conditioned and there were no freeways? I wonder if they were trying to get me to make the decision to stay in California. They liked it when I was the one to make decisions about my life.

My birthday was June 4th and I turned fourteen. I wore patent leather high-heeled shoes—moderately high, anyway—not knowing that my feet would swell on the ride through three days of sweltering summer heat and the shoes would become instruments of torture. Night and day we traveled through Arizona and New Mexico and eventually we came to El Paso. When everyone got out for a bus break, I was feeling nauseated and didn't want to eat. I did, however, want to go down the street where the pretty shops were. After looking at jewelry and clothes for a while, I turned back, just as I saw a bus pulling out with the word DALLAS on the front. I ran as fast as I could and the driver let me on. Why he did that, I can't imagine because he must have known that the bus I was supposed to be on was still at the restaurant. I had a ticket for the express bus; this one took the milk run. Many hours after I was supposed to be in Dallas, I was still bumping along as slowly as if I were on a mule train.

My Great-Aunt Mamie was supposed to meet me at the bus station in Dallas when I arrived. When I wasn't on the bus, it didn't occur to her to call my parents. She just went back to her office downtown and waited for me to show up. Which I did. Great-Aunt Mamie was a jeweler and a watchmaker before she went into real estate and I remember walking into her office looking like I'd walked all the way from LA.

"Well, here you are!" she said, so glad to see me and I even got a big hug in spite of my sweaty, dirty and bedraggled appearance. "I knew you'd show up eventually."

It seemed that every member of my family thought I was capable of taking care of myself. During that summer I stayed with one aunt or another, one friend or another and no one ever kept track of where I was.

What were they thinking!

Everything in my childhood set me up to believe that all things were possible and I could create any life I wanted if I was willing to work for it. One might argue that this is not categorically true, of course, but that perception certainly trained me to know I was responsible for my choices and there was no one else to blame if things turned out badly.

There were numerous requirements to my parent's approval, however, and while they gave my life direction, there was a downside. I was expected to do work that was important and valuable. I had to be willing to work as hard as the task required and not give up when things were challenging. I had to be brave and not be daunted by rejection or criticism. I had to remember that my word was my bond. No pressure, right? Do you think their expectations, or my interpretation of them, might have had something to do with the migraine headaches I had from the age of four?

When I was very young—seven or eight or nine—I knew I would be a writer. I remember my first submission to a magazine. I was standing at a mailbox in my Brownie uniform with a torn sash on the left side and dropping my poems in the mail slot. Then came one of the most helpful things my mother ever said to me: "Now, you know, Sweet Girl, they don't allow you to be a writer until you've collected many rejection slips." When the inevitable rejection came, I celebrated. I had earned my very first one. I no longer celebrate rejection but I don't let it draw blood, either.

I was alone a lot in those early days. After school I couldn't go home until my dad had finished his work because we lived too far away and besides no one was home. It was a blessing really and one of the reasons I became a writer. The school library was my haven. I would sit alone and read book after book and sometimes I would write my own.

In the summertime, when I was a little older, I stayed home and listened to soap operas. I would write a script for the next day and pretend it was my own show. Sometimes I imagined I was playing one of the roles. Always, I was the writer. This was undoubtedly one of the things that motivated me to have my own radio show in Los Angeles when I was nineteen. I had a fifteen-minute radio program for children, dramatizing stories from the Bible that ran for twenty-six weeks on an AM station that had the unfortunate name of KFVD. I wrote the scripts, dramatized all the parts as the storyteller, got a sponsor (The National Council of Churches) and the radio station gave the time as a public service. I also picked the music. I even wrote my own fan letters on different sizes and colors of papers because I didn't think anyone else would write to me. I wanted to seem popular so my contract would be renewed. No wonder the station manager always had a twinkle in his eyes when I went to work. He never let me know he suspected a thing. And my contract was renewed for another thirteen weeks.

Before I found the sponsor, I tried a more commercial route. I lugged a heavy tape recorder all over town to try to get some company to support my program. I never made an appointment—just walked in. Would they like to hear some of the show? Some managers would let me play part of the tape and make my pitch—surely just out of curiosity or kindness. I told them the advantages of institutional advertising but that approach didn't work out too well. Why didn't I know that car dealerships and fancy dress shops weren't likely sponsors of a religious program for children on Sunday mornings? I don't remember discussing my business plan with my parents. Surely they would have given me better advice. Well, I was just eighteen when I began trying to sell the show and maybe they thought I should figure it out for myself.

The radio show ran for twenty-six weeks and then my attention began to wane. I decided to write a screenplay. How did I know how to write a screenplay, you may ask? I did not. However, I began. A little research about structure and form and many hours with buns to chair, and I was finished.

Without contacts in Hollywood I set out to sell my story. How is it possible that tenacity got me into the doors of the William Morris Agency, one of the best in town? It is not possible, not realistic, not believable, but it happened. An agent actually read my screenplay! I was still nineteen and sure that my career was on its way. I must have amused this serious big-desked, pipe-smoking man because he actually called me into his office when he finished. This is very close to the actual words he said: "Your characters are well developed, your dialogue is pretty good but that's the most ridiculous plot I've ever read! Write what you know!"

That's when I decided to be an actress.

This was not at all the kind of career my parents had in mind. Of course , I still wanted to be a writer but that could come later. When I auditioned for local stage shows, I usually got the parts. Maybe it would be that easy to be cast in the movies. I was not lacking in confidence.

Over the next five years, and against all odds, I was an actress in six movies and even costarred in a few. They were all bad. Once I played the romantic lead opposite Dana Andrews; he was terrible and I was worse. A reviewer said, "Miss Earle gave a wooden performance of truly Redwoodian proportion." He was right. My only defense is that I was almost six months pregnant and we should have finished the film before I blossomed. But as things are wont to go, the film started shooting later than planned and ran longer than expected. I kept my weight down but my expanding abdomen meant I got only close-ups toward the end. The problem was with my newly acquired chipmunk cheeks— they really didn't add much to my image of a romantic lead. When I finally kissed Dana Andrews in front of the projected Lincoln Monument and the movie was a wrap, I think everyone was relieved. Of course, a little pregnancy doesn't excuse the acting, and for that I have no defense at all. Hollywood did not suffer a great loss when I quit to be a mom.

The Past is the Mother
of the Future

There's nothing like an ecumenical family to raise a liberal child. When I was growing up in the suburbs of Dallas, the family used to come for Sunday supper. There were my parents (Methodist), my grandmother (Episcopalian), my Uncle Orville (Catholic), my Uncle Frank (Baptist), and my Great-Aunt Mamie (Agnostic). They all had strong feelings about their beliefs, all talked at once, yet everyone seemed to know what everyone else had said.

My father, who was a quiet, Texas Ranger sort of man, didn't join in very much and Great-Aunt Mamie tormented the rest of them by refusing to agree with anyone.

I found the conversations fascinating and very early on I came to the conclusion that a lot of good people could feel sure they were right about God even when none of them agreed. Those Sunday suppers prepared me to become ecumenical. I was always curious about the One I couldn't see. I might not know much about Him, but I was sure He knew everything about me. It never occurred to me that 'He' might be a 'She' and imagining an energy that had no discernable shape was way beyond my comprehension.

My Uncle Frank was a Baptist minister and a kind, delightful man until he got to the pulpit. Then he took on some other voice and roared and yelled at people and sounded like one of those fire and brimstone preachers. I was maybe seven, or could have been eight, and I really did not like his sermons. I would hear him rehearsing them and it didn't sound like my real uncle. (The one I loved who was so good to me.) I told him God could hear him quite well and he didn't have to shout. I could hear him all the way from the church to the parsonage next door where I stayed with my grandmother. On Sundays, I would tell him what was wrong with his sermons and he didn't like that. Finally, he called my mother and told her to tell me to stop criticizing everything he said in church.

Mother drove all the way from Dallas to the little town of Hutchins and talked privately with me about matters of respect. I said Frank was all wrong about God. Which shows you just how tolerant I was! Even so, she said I couldn't talk that way anymore. I had to be polite. But when she left and I didn't like Frank's interpretation of Scripture, I thought it was my duty to tell him he was wrong. Hadn't my parents always taught me to stand up for what I believe?

So after one particularly flamboyant sermon, I thought he missed the whole point of the Bible and felt morally obligated to defend God's honor. "God is *love*," I said angrily. Didn't he know that? I stated my position and he matched me rage for rage when he said: "Little girl, *your arms are too short to box with God!*"

I gave my uncle quite a bit of credit for the cleverness of that phrase until, years later, I discovered that his punch line was from a poem by James Weldon Johnson, included in a book of 'Negro' sermons published in 1927. Eventually it became the title of a Broadway musical. At that point, I blamed him for plagiarism as well as fanaticism.

When I told that story a few years ago, someone said, "That must have made you feel like you were really insignificant." Of course it didn't. If a little girl like me could upset that big, loud man and make my mother drive all the way from Dallas because he was afraid of my opinion, I must have been a pretty powerful kid. Got a little ego going there, didn't I?

I was a very spiritual child, despite the fact that I wasn't siding with any one perspective, and frequently joined the supper debates with firm convictions. I was grateful for the beautiful Methodist Church with the tall steeple and programs for kids in the summers. The minister knew I wanted to be a writer and one summer he gave me my own column in the church paper. I even had a byline. On hot summer nights, they showed movies on the lawn. We tolerated chiggers biting our ankles and mosquitoes nibbling on bare arms. There were ping-pong tables and games and it was the only interesting thing happening in our part of town. I'm sure it drew more kids to church than the sermons that tended to run long.

In spite of my ongoing argument with others on the nature of the Divine, I believed just one thing: I was put on this earth for a purpose and it was my job to find out what that was. My very friendly God would help me, but I had to do the work myself. My mother also taught me that if I didn't use my "gifts" they would be taken away. How I reconciled that threat with a loving God is difficult to understand. But I'm sure that philosophy had a great deal to do with my relentless work ethic and a need to succeed, which on occasion, has bordered on the neurotic.

One year when I was in elementary school, I "published" a newspaper. Of course I had no way of duplicating anything so I carefully typed several copies with the hunt and peck method on an old school typewriter. I used my father's Kodak camera to take the candid snapshots and white library paste to stick them to the pages of the next edition. The papers were passed around from one student to another and all of them wanted to read it to see if I wrote anything about them. That was the year that writing became my addiction of choice. I'll have to admit that it was many years before I found an audience as enthusiastic as that one.

In the summers, I spent many hours in the house alone with no one close by to play with. My chores at home were not demanding; it was up to me to keep the dining room in perfect condition, to set the mahogany table with my great-grandmothers silver and to be sure candles were ready for lighting. It pleased my parents when I dressed the table with some interesting centerpieces. Our dinners were always rather formal, unless on occasion we ate in the kitchen and then my mother called that "eating pig fashion." I could even put a bottle of milk on the table on these occasions. No butter was available during the war but something that was white as snow in a plastic bag was the substitute. There was a big yellow blob in the middle of the "butter" and I had to knead it until all of the package was a golden color.

Regular dolls held very little fascination for me. However, my mother's collection of perfume bottles became perfect characters for my plays. Her silver jewelry case with beautiful colored stones became a throne of encrusted rubies and emeralds. How easily one could choose the king, the queen, the young princess, and clever jester, the evil duke. Cardboard boxes, one atop the other, were the foundation for the castle. Sometimes, the bottles were kids, just my age. Like actors, the bottles could easily change roles. Scraps of velvet or lace from mother's sewing box made fine costumes and hour after hour, I watched my stories come to life on this stage.

I would listen to soap-operas on the radio and that was the highlight of my day. I would listen to "Ma Perkins, or "Stella Dallas," then write a script for the following episode. It was great training and helped me develop a good ear for dialogue and a mind for story. Of course, when you live in Texas, coming up with stories is pretty much like breathing air. It's the basic rule of civilized conversation in Dallas, and you'd best be on your toes to tell a good one before someone else jumps in ahead of you.

I was fourteen when I won my first writing award. That was for an essay contest on some aspect of the Constitution. It was my first "professional" success and you would have thought I'd won a scholarship to Harvard, that's how happy I was.

It's that first sweet taste of success that can set the pattern for a lifetime. Writing was the most satisfying thing in the world to me. I played with words instead of dolls. In my diary, there was a place for new words that I thought were powerful. Like *pungent*. Words that gave me shivers, like *abandoned*. Or made me laugh, like *rambunctious* or *portly*. Words were like friends, only more available.

Writing screenplays was another great pleasure. Tarzan was my hero and, although I had no idea how to write a screenplay, pages were filled with the adventures of this powerful man and his Lady Jane. There were lots of scenes where they swung bravely from tree to tree, over swamps and deep canyons and they weren't even afraid of the alligators that were just waiting for them to fall.

During my life with Leonard, I was out of touch with myself as a writer. I was busy being a bride, then a mom and a hostess, all the while trying to educate myself in the subjects that interested Leonard and his friends. (This was in the 50's, which explains a lot.) But to tell you the truth, it was pretty wonderful. I didn't want to act anymore and was too busy to write. Life was full and about as perfect as I could imagine.

Years later, after Al and I married, I started writing again, a few magazine articles and song lyrics that became an anthem, *The Morning Star*. The music was composed by Paul Sjolund. Then I wrote about my feelings and my family and my unusual life choices. For years, these writings went into a box called *Someday*.

In 1971, I was asked to be the Director of Creative Worship at my church and from that moment on, everything changed in my life. The committee included some of the finest talents in Hollywood. Steve Allen, who was not only a brilliant comedian, he was just plain brilliant. Film producer,

Jim Collier, composer/conductor Keith Clarke (who went on to conduct the Vienna Symphony Orchestra), Paul Bergen with his magnificent voice and of course, Marge Champion, who is one of the great dancers of the MGM musicals. There were others too. Less famous but really creative. There was a lot of talent at the Bel Air Presbyterian Church.

We were not critical of the traditional worship service. This was not a protest against anything; it was an embracing of possibilities. What if those who chose to, could be more involved in experiential worship? What if we went back to the oldest traditions of ancient Hebrews, early Christians? What if we followed these threads and the significance of them into the present? What would that look like? How would that feel?

"King David danced before the Lord with all his might," the Scriptures say, and so it was with Jews and early Christians. And so it was at our church one Sunday night when we invited a rabbi and a group of Yemenite Israeli dancers to show us how David might have expressed praise in movement. After a deeply moving experience in liturgical dance, they led the congregation to the parking lot, where car lights formed a huge circle. Within it, Jews taught Christians to dance the Hora, a traditional folk dance where young people and old celebrated with great enthusiasm. And in our predominately Jewish neighborhood, Jews came out to see what the Christians were doing with their music. Oh, what a lovely time it was.

Many of the elements we used are common now in many different churches and synagogues but in 1971, they were quite shocking to some parishioners.

I discovered John West at Saint Andrews Benedictine Monastery, in Valyermo, California, at a fascinating festival of art, music, dance and spiritual happenings. I walked past a raised platform and saw this beautiful black man expressing his faith through dance, using the Barbara Streisand recording of the Lord's Prayer. I was deeply moved and asked John to come to Bel Air and dance for the congregation. Then I asked

Marge to dance with him. This lovely man and the tiny, elegant dancer were the first to bring sacred dance to this community. Oh, it was a fine moment. And that's just a very small part of what *Catch the New Wind* is about.

We praised God with primitive African instruments. We took communion by candlelight in small groups that gathered and broke homemade bread while elders and children read poetry with flutes and cellos in accompaniment. This is just a blink of the beauty that unfolded. I could write a whole book about it. Well, I did, in fact. I asked Marge Champion to collaborate with me and she agreed. At that time, the ideal publisher for this kind of material was Word Books. I showed our photographs and discussed the concept with Floyd Thatcher, their Editor and Chief. He was excited about it and we had a contract before the book was even finished.

What a glorious feeling it was to open the mail box one morning and find a copy of *Catch the New Wind: the Church is Alive and Dancing.* It was 1972.

The fact that the subject matter was dear to my heart made it even more special. And working with Marge Champion, one of my closest friends since 1959, made the journey even better.

How was it possible to have an appropriate celebration? We dismissed all the fine restaurants that came to mind; then it was Marge who had the solution. We had a picnic at Griffith Park. Al brought a rare bottle of 1929 French Burgundy that was liquid velvet, having been in the cask until it was bottled a few years before. I brought Waterford crystal glasses and all the table trimmings. Gower brought Russian caviar that was impossible to get in those times. Marge brought four second-row-center tickets to the last performance of Neal Diamond's concert, *Hot August Night.* Let me tell you, dear reader, it does not get better than that.

Barbara Walters was hosting the Today Show at the time

our book was published and when she read, *Catch the New Wind*, Barbara wanted to interview us on the show. If you're not a film buff or old enough to know about Marge, it's enough to know that she and her husband, Gower Champion, were a very famous dancing team. They danced at a command performance for the Queen of England and for three US Presidents and were on all the important variety shows on TV. When she was thirteen, Walt Disney hired her to be the model for Snow White. Marge would dance and artists would create their magic and when you watch that film, you see an animated version of Marge. Now in her nineties, she is still dancing, still performing.

Barbara Walters introduced us both on the *Today Show*, and then Marge (without John West, I'm sorry to say) performed that beautiful sacred dance. I was sitting next to Barbara, and I saw tears surface while she watched but they were gone by the time the camera turned back on us. While Marge caught her breath, Barbara began the interview with me. She said, "Marilee, what makes you think this kind of worship is right for everybody?"

"I don't think *anything* is right for everybody, Barbara. But some people don't feel at home with traditional hymns. They find it hard to relate to some of the lyrics. Sermons may sound like lectures to those who long for a more experiential form of worship." Then, Marge joined us and we had thirteen minutes on the show, which was really exciting. The sad part was that not one copy of our book had yet arrived in a bookstore on the East Coast.

When I was invited to the Vatican the following year, Cardinal Wright, who was head of all education for the Catholic Church, said the Pope wanted to know what I thought of the Jazz Mass. I thought it was quite an honor for a Presbyterian woman to be asked such a question by the Pope. Cardinal Wright said the celebrations in the book were "inspired" and I can't think of a higher complement than that.

Marge and I were interviewed by *Newsweek* and it was easier to explain our philosophy to the Pope than to the reporter. He was a charming man and obviously struggled to understand the significance of a foot-washing ceremony in a denomination that didn't do that. Then, I tried to explain the historical meaning of liturgical dance as a way to praise God. I wish he could actually have witnessed a ceremony. It was a good article, but not as long as it might have been if he had experienced it himself.

Marge and I travelled to many places across the country and it was terrific working in churches, and an occasional synagogue, helping communities explore their own creativity and consider non-traditional ways to express their faith.

From Kennedy Center
to Jerusalem

In the 1950's, Carol Lawrence was the first to play the role of Maria in the Broadway production of *Westside Story*. Years later in 1978, she was planning to tour with an inspirational one-woman-show and I was asked to write the words—or the *book*, as it's called for the production. Ron Harris would compose the music. I was given no direction other than the date when I had to deliver the script. I thought it would be interesting for Carol to play a different kind of Maria, and I began researching the character I had in mind.

I decided to set the story in Israel and title it *Someone Special*. It is the story of a young girl who was only thirteen, pregnant, and feeling the anxiety any unmarried girl would feel who lived in a culture that could very well have stoned her for the perceived offense. What was stronger than her anxiety, however, was the power of the Angel who had came to tell her she would be the mother of the Christ child.

I began the story at that point. Half way through the program, time shifted. Carol transformed herself into the elderly Mary, who had lost her son on a Roman cross. She made this change on stage, using the costume as a device for her transition. The top layer of her costume, a rich blue, was lined with a more somber shade of burgundy and with a slow and graceful movement, Carol lifted the back of the overskirt to create a hood as her body suddenly hunched forward, her voice deepened and aged. In that moment, she appeared to be a very old woman. This earthy, Jewish Mary was wise and strong and she brought many in the audience to laughter when she sang "The Kitchen Song" and to tears when she sang of her longing for her son. Certain lines I wrote then are particularly meaningful to me now— *"I've tasted a little from every cup and grown through the struggles. I've loved until I ached from loving, and wept until my heart was sick of tears. I have known life in all its complexities—and looking back, I would not undo one moment if I could."*

One of Carol's first performances was at the Dorothy Chandler Pavilion in Los Angeles with Andre Previn conducting the orchestra. Nancy Reagan saw the show and arranged a performance in Washington. She sent engraved invitations to the members of Congress to be her guest at a special performance of *Someone Special* at Kennedy Center in Washington. There was no charge for the evening performance and no one would be admitted without an invitation.

There was one little problem. Nothing "religious" is allowed to be presented at the Kennedy Center. There was a huge buzz about this in Washington and my phone started ringing. The Washington Post wanted an interview. Tickets were very much in demand since there were more invitations mailed than there are seats at the theater and there was great curiosity about why the First Lady was sending the invitations.

I would be inclined to call this subject religious, although it was surely a non-traditional presentation. But if the First Lady of the United States had arranged for this performance and invited members of Congress to see it, I wasn't about to interfere. Finally, Mary of Nazareth was considered an historical figure and the show could go on.

Al and I held a dinner for our guests at the Watergate Hotel, which was in itself quite an experience after all its notoriety. Then a limousine took us on the short ride to the theater.

There wasn't an empty seat in the house; each one was

filled with members of Congress and their significant others. Al and I were there with Tamara and my mother, plus Leonard's brother, Arnold Picker, who was vice-president of United Artists with his wife, Ruth. Lou Evans Jr., minister of the National Presbyterian Church, was there, too. Our history goes way back, for he is the man who baptized Leonard and our children, buried my father, and then in 1962 he married Al and me. His wife, Colleen Townsend Evans was there with him. She has been one of my dearest friends for more than fifty years. Barbara Goldsmith, author of many books, flew down from New York and you can imagine how excited I was that evening

And then the performance began.

And then it was over.

The next morning, the Washington Post devoted several long columns and a huge drawing of Mary holding her baby Jesus that covered half the length of the page. But this wasn't religious, you understand.

The reviewer was much kinder than I would have been if I had been the one to judge the evening. I would have had to say that the orchestra was wonderful, Carol's voice was beautiful, the costume was unique, the audience appreciative. But it wasn't Carol's finest hour. If tears come from an actor before the audience feels them rising within themselves, the audience has their release. Better for an actor to fight the tears and let the audience be the ones to cry—or at least try not to. I understand why Carol wouldn't accept my direction, after all, she was the one with the most experience and I'm a writer not a director. But never mind. We had a terrific time in DC. As far as I know, there never were any complaints about the nature of the material. It was, as they said—historical.

About that time, Floyd Thatcher, editor of two of my early works, said he would like to publish the text of *Someone*

Special as a book. Great idea, I thought and had a strong feeling that the words should be superimposed over photographs of the textures in the land of Israel. No people, no buildings, nothing that might not have been seen by that young Mary. As a proposal, I took pictures of old stone steps, cumulous clouds and sandy dunes near Los Angeles and proposed a layout for the book. I also suggested that Floyd send a photographer to Israel or hire one who lived there to take the pictures. Floyd called and said he wanted *me* to go to Israel and take the pictures!

I have had very little instruction in photography but I have a good eye and had a clear vision of how I wanted the book to look. And to tell you the entire truth, I must say that I shot sixteen hundred photographs of Israel in three weeks when only about forty were needed in the book. Using two Nikons, three lenses, a sturdy tripod and a good lab man, I could hardly miss.

It was terribly cold that January. Al couldn't go with me because he had babies to deliver too close to my travel dates. I asked a friend, Barbara Carlsberg, if she would like to go with me and she agreed.

Political tensions were high in Israel at that time and we flew El Al because of their excellent security. We arrived late at night, in the pouring rain, and it was Shabbat, Saturday, the Holy day of the week for Jews. No cars, not even taxis were allowed in the old part of the city. A friend had suggested we stay in a crusader castle that was adapted for tourists where we would meet interesting travelers who preferred a non-hotel. I didn't know what that meant but it sounded like an interesting thing to do.

So the taxi took us as far as they were allowed to go and then we walked a short distance to the castle. I carried twenty-five pounds of camera equipment and thirteen pounds of clothes and personal items. When we arrived at the ancient building late at night, a note was on the entry door telling us the number of our room. We wandered the hall until we found it. There was no heat. It was just as cold inside as it was outside, only without the rain.

Barbara looked at me quizzically, hunkered down in her coat, "And why is it that we're not staying at the King David Hotel?"

"Good question. But, hey, we have layers of clothes and blankets and you're used to camping, so at least we have good beds!" Neither of us rushed to test them.

There was no restaurant at this non-hotel and we were both starving. It was far past the dinner hour but we thought we might find something open, so we went out in the rain again and down the street for some food and a glass or two of wine. Although it was late in the evening, the streets were bustling with people, and soldiers carrying guns. I'm not accustomed to guns and have a deep distrust of anyone holding one. Especially Uzzi's that look as potentially deadly as they actually are. There were so many soldiers you would have thought you were on an army base. Or in the middle of a war.

We found a restaurant and went in out of the cold. No sooner had we ordered drinks than two Uzzi-carrying soldiers approached the table. "What are your names," they asked.

We told them.

"Why are you in Israel?"

We told them that too.

"Where are you staying?"

At this point, I was getting nervous. I hoped my voice wasn't trembling.

What had we done wrong? Why were they interrogating us? I was very uncomfortable.

Then suddenly, they just sat down at the empty chairs by our table and I started thinking that this was really strange. One was smiling and asking questions about America and our trip and where we planned to go and then it occurred to me— these guys weren't interrogating us, they were trying to pick us up!

Now you may be reading this and thinking we were rather naïve and unseasoned about either the culture or men in general but if you had been there, you would have seen how serious they were. Have you ever seen an Uzzi? It's *big*. That is one serious looking sub-machine gun and they were handling it so carelessly. But we were being on our best social behavior and as gracious as either of us could be, which probably gave the wrong impression. One turned to me and said, straight out of the blue: "Would you like to go dancing?"

"I can't go dancing with you, I'm married!" I heard myself say.

"Madam, I don't want to marry you, I just want to take you dancing!"

I think I heard Bob Hope say that same line years ago, even so, it was startling in this context.

It was a quick dinner and firm good-by, then Barbara and I headed back to our room that was colder than any I ever slept in, a situation that did not bring out the best in me. I grumbled a lot. I longed for a hot bath after traveling all the way from L.A., but I wasn't about to take a shower in a stone room with no heater.

The next day was no warmer, nor the next. At night we slept under all the covers we could gather, with our wool caps, leather gloves and socks besides. Al had bought me a small package that he said would keep me warm; it had something to do with space travel and reminded me of a very large silver gum wrapper and was just as thin. It was supposed to keep body heat in. The problem was, I kept changing position to try and get warm, while the strange thin 'blanket' made a loud crackling sound every time I moved. And Barbara, who must have a different internal thermostat, was still as a mouse and finally called from her narrow twin bed for me to quit wiggling so we could both get some sleep.

As promised, we did meet some interesting people in this strange facility, and one of them suggested we go to a *Mikvah*.

"You'll surely get warm there," she suggested and another girl explained that these were natural underground hot springs that had pools in various degrees of heat. It sounded great to me—I envisioned an Elizabeth Arden spa.

"It's a place for ritual bathing," she said. Whatever that meant.

Later in the day, the three of us went together and I could just imagine these great caves under the old city of Jerusalem. I couldn't wait. I could almost feel the large heated towel scented with lavender, or some exotic flower. I asked where we could get a cab, but our new friend was shocked. "Oh, no, we take the bus. It is much too expensive to take a cab!"

Well, when in Rome (or in Jerusalem) do as others do. I didn't want to offend her by pushing the situation and I try very hard not to travel like the "ugly American" who shows off by spending carelessly. So we took the bus. And walked quite a long way.

Finally, at the *Mikvah*, an attendant took our purses and put them behind the desk. I was very aware that my passport and all my travelers checks were in that purse, but I couldn't very well take them into the water so—ah well. We took off our clothes and put them on a bench. We were stark naked just like all the women there. But two skinny, American women who both looked Irish, seemed to attract quite a bit of attention. That part wasn't so comfortable. We entered the first cave. It was so wonderfully hot and steam was rising from the pool, dozens of naked women relaxed in the hot water, a few young children wandering around, then a dog or two. I thought of Fellini. He could make a fascinating movie in this place. Then I remembered to ask, "What's a ritual bath?"

Our friend said this is the area in Jerusalem where the Hassidic Jews live and after menses, every woman must come to the baths before she returns to her husband. I was fascinated by the mood of the cave, or series of caves. You don't really have to know a language to know when women are talking just the same way we do at home, you'd hear laughter, someone calling to her child, a dog whining, someone upset and telling others what happened to make her feel so distraught. The language was strange to me, but there was something quite familiar about women sharing their stories with other women. The tone in any language is exactly the same. I liked this place for the communion of women almost as much as I did for this nest of warmth in a very cold land.

I remember seeing a woman who could have walked straight out of a Renoir painting, with her long golden-red hair cascading down her very plump body. (About 250 pounds of plump, I guessed.) What is she doing? I wondered as she sat on a stone bench by a small pool. Then I realized that she was shaving a very personal area of her body! She was just as nonchalant as if that weren't a rather private thing to do. Well, who's to say what's private and what isn't? Who made me the judge of propriety in a culture on the other side of the planet?

Barbara and I were finally ready to leave the warmth of the *Mikvah* and head back to the ancient castle, our non-hotel. Our new friend would stay awhile to talk with someone she knew. We dressed, reclaimed our purses and asked the attendant for a cab. Okay, is it called a *cab* in Jerusalem? No. Is it a *taxi*? How would you say taxi in Hebrew? Or Yiddish? How would you describe it if you were playing charades?

Finally, we gave up and walked toward the bus stop. Only somehow we got lost. A man walked toward us. Most Israeli's speak English and are very helpful, so I said, "Excuse me, sir..." He hurried past. Hassidic, I figured. Apparently, he was one whose practice of faith doesn't allow him to speak to strange women. We wandered on and soon were just as cold as we were before we arrived at the baths. It took a while, but finally we found our way to the bus and arrived back at our non-hotel. Under our mounds of clothing, with teeth chattering and feet freezing, we once again tried to sleep.

After a while, we decided to take the advice of Heim Hefer, who was the Consul General of Israel in Los Angeles, and stay at the American Colony Hotel, which was once the home of Lawrence of Arabia and had not only beautiful architecture, but heat! And a bar besides. In the tiny bar, Barbara and I ordered beer because—I'm sorry, but in Israel wine is not their most outstanding product. Soon the small area was full of people and everybody talked to everybody. I had my own plan: I would talk with anyone but I always paid for my own drinks and I never left the room with anyone. No problem. We met the most interesting people and I loved the history of the hotel and the journalists with their stories of adventures in exotic places. The ambiance made it all seem more like a dream or a movie than just one more night on a professional assignment.

There was so much about that trip to Israel that was fascinating. We stayed in a kibbutz on the sea of Galilee, met Mordici Artzielli, a journalist in the Negev, who later came to LA with his wife and daughter and I introduced them to my husband.

On the kibbutz, Barbara went into the lounge and a man offered to buy her a beer. It seemed harmless enough and it was a good thing to get to talk with the local people. It seemed uneventful until late that night when someone knocked on our door and we knew enough not to open it. I called security while Barbara told the man to leave us alone. In moments, Israelis were there and, from the window, Barbara recognized the man she had talked with in the bar.

The next day, I told our guide about it and when I mentioned that the man had bought Barbara a beer, he was visibly shaken.

"She let him buy her a beer?" he asked as if this was some terrible thing to do. "He was Arab?"

I nodded. "It was just a beer! It meant nothing."

"It was a contract."

I was totally confused.

"When she accepted the offer, she was agreeing to much more than a beer."

After I got through thinking how ridiculous that was, I realized that when you don't know the customs of a country, you may be committing yourself to things you would never agree to. We were grateful to the Israeli security on the kibbutz and were much more careful after that.

I saw Israel with one eye shut, the other looking through the lens of the camera. But I loved the people and the beauty of the land. In the news, Israel can look rocky and barren; but when you stand there in real life, it is magical with its stark beauty. Even before I left, I wanted to come back. I wanted to bring Al there someday.

Late one afternoon, Barbara and I climbed to the top of Masada, where thousands of years ago, courageous Jews made a stand again the Roman army. When the end was close, they took their own lives, choosing death over Roman domination. The ruins of the village remain. On this day, the place was empty of tourists. The silence was more than silence and time seemed endless. We were alone, just the two of us on top of the mountain, wandering through stones of history. Then we heard a terrifying noise and looked up to see two phantom jets swooping down on us, just to see if we were causing trouble. You can't hear phantom jets approaching and then you hear more than you ever want to hear, right over your head. Apparently, we looked harmless for after the dive, they flew on their way.

The morning we left Israel, we arrived at the airport early, having heard that going through customs and security can take quite a while. Which is a gross understatement. I can now tell you, from personal experience—I know why the airports are so safe in Israel.

A woman searched my luggage. A man asked many questions. Where had we stayed in Jerusalem? Well, at the American Colony, which, by now I knew, was Arab territory. It was recommended to me by Haime Heffer, who was not only a diplomat but a famous Israeli poet. Even so, we probably should have chosen the King David Hotel. And there was the matter of my coat. On the outside, it looked like a traditional trench coat, albeit burgundy in color. On the inside, my mother had modified the lining. She was concerned that my purse would be stolen while I was shooting so, here's how it looked: There was a pocket for my passport, another for my money, one for a guide book, another for lipstick and comb, there was…well, I looked like a watch salesman at a border town. It made that woman in security very suspicious. I was properly searched and then the almost-worst thing happened. Al had given me one of the first mini-tape recorders, a thing the woman had never seen. It took some time for her to be comfortable with the fact that it was only a recorder, not a device to be used with ill intentions. Then she took the lens off my camera and started to stick her finger inside the body of the Nikon when I yelled, "Don't do that! You'll ruin my camera." I guess I was rather loud. Men showed up all around me. They looked at my coat, my recorder, my lenses. At me. They did not like what they saw.

"Please," I said, "I'll miss my plane!"

"Don't worry," the woman said.

I thought she meant that El Al tends to run late. Actually, she meant it wouldn't do me any good to be upset because there was nothing I could do about it anyway. It took some time. Many questions. Finally, they agreed that I was not a terrorist and let me pass. I looked for Barbara. Then I realized my plane was on its way to London. Barbara was apparently on the plane and she had made the hotel reservation in London, and I didn't know where we were staying. I had a tizzy-fit as only an age-regressing, highly frustrated, intensely emotional, terrible actress can throw. It wasn't pretty. I so rarely lose my temper and I still don't know how to do it with style.

The Israelis were very accommodating. The uniformed

person called the tower-person who called the pilot, who asked the steward, who asked Barbara, who told the steward, who told the pilot, who told the tower-person who told the uniformed person who told me: "It's the Xytbvws Hotel." Did you ever play 'gossip' or "telephone" when you were a kid? It all sounded like gobble-dee-gook to me. Many hours later I arrived at Heathrow, resisted taking the train into London (which would have been faster and much cheaper) but I splurged on a cab and guessed at the name of the hotel. It wasn't the name they told me, but miracle of miracles that's where she was. At some deep level, I must have known the name, I just allowed the name of the hotel to slip from my subconscious mind across my corpus callosum into conscious awareness. All was well. And in spite of all the incidents, and perhaps because of some of them, I dearly love Israel. I bought a gold charm with the words "Pray for peace in Jerusalem." And I do.

Tonight I'm thinking about that trip to Israel and how intriguing it all seemed. Was it such a wild adventure, after all? Maybe not for some who are more worldly, more traveled than I. It's not a big deal in these days, maybe it wasn't in those days either, but it was both challenging and empowering for me to be on assignment in Israel.

Would I do that now? Would I dust off my camera or buy a new one? Travel alone or with a friend? Where would I go and what story would I tell? There's an idea in there somewhere; I'll keep an open mind and see where it leads me.

A few weeks ago, about ten in the morning, I'm walking toward a bookstore on State Street in Santa Barbara when all of a sudden, I trip on nothing at all and fall hard on the sidewalk. This is a small incident in reality but a huge one in my perspective of my situation. For the first time I acknowledge that I am not as I used to be. I did not always trip on air, and my vulnerability could hold me back from the adventurous life I long to enjoy.

The fall is totally my fault because I'm not paying attention. My face is bleeding a little, nothing bad, but its scraped all over one side of my cheek. My temple and cheekbone are tender to the touch, which will probably become a flaming black eye by morning. My right knee hurts a lot and there are soon to be bruises from my knee to my ankle. The top of a perfectly good pair of shoes is scraped to the lining, no longer wearable and my car keys are somewhere in the gutter.

Two kind girls come running and fuss over me like I am some old woman. One finds my keys; the other gently dusts dirt from my face. They are so sweet and seem reluctant to leave me. I want to go home but I know better than to drive when I feel so shaken, so I walk to the bookstore, order a cappuccino and wait until I feel steady. Then I buy the book I want and drive home.

It all makes me feel so fragile. What if I had been alone in Bali or Paris, or Prague? I run my hand gently across my face and feel the roughened surface of my skin. The area of my temple is the most tender. What if the fall had been harder, if I had been unconscious? If no one had come. What would have happened to me then?

I have never been afraid to travel alone, not until this moment. Suddenly, I feel old and dependent. Fragile. It makes me want to cry, but that would surely give credence to the fear, so I fight against the feeling.

When I get home, I call Gina, in Arizona. I want to hear her voice but decide not to tell her what happened. I don't want her to worry. But as soon as she says, "How are you?" I tell the whole story.

She says "Oh, Mom, no matter where you were, someone would have helped you up and you would have met some new friends who probably would have invited you for a glass of wine and after a few hours of good stories, they would have asked you out to dinner. You would have been fine!"

She's right. Of course she is. I'll always be fine, if I believe I am.

So now I repeat my mantra like a child saying her nightly prayers: "Whatever happens, I'll deal with it."

I curl into bed with a recent gift from my dear friend, Cleo Baldon: (don't laugh) a teddy bear that's filled with lavender! (Okay, laugh. Why not?) It goes in the microwave and stays hot for hours even on a cold night like this. I cuddle the warmth of it as my mind is comforted by memories of long ago.

I remember when an aftershock of the Northridge earthquake rocked our house and Al pushed me against a corner and covered me with his body. I remember how he rubbed my head when I had a migraine.

I remembered other things as well.

Good night, Love.

The Gift of Knowing

In 1981, Boris Sagal was in Israel directing Peter O'Toole and Peter Strauss in the miniseries, *Masada*. It is a tragic, courageous story with a huge cast and difficult working conditions. When Marge Champion, (no longer married to Gower Champion, now the wife of Boris.) invited us to come to Israel and visit them, Al and I were both excited to go.

We went to the usual tourist spots, knowing full well that the Holy Sights had moved closer and closer to the main road as the years passed. That made no difference to us—whether the Christ Child was born in the cave that had all the candles and ceremony, or in the one across the next hill, seemed irrelevant. Anywhere in that part of Israel, you can feel the dramatic scope of the land and imagine what it might have been like to travel to Jerusalem from Nazareth in those days when Rome dictated life and death on a whim.

When we arrived at the base of Masada, the production was in a typical flurry of activity. Something had gone wrong, as it often does, particularly when there is a huge cast and some are speaking Hebrew, some English, some Arabic and you're on location on a remote mountaintop. Boris had his hands full and was greatly distracted. I don't remember seeing much of him the entire trip. I do remember when we visited the set and Al sat down in an empty chair. He didn't notice that it was the director's chair and absolutely nobody on a set sits down in the director's throne, even if it is made of canvas. Of course, Al had no way of knowing the significance of that. The crew must have thought Al was the "angel" who financed the picture since he so casually usurped the sacred seat. It was tantamount to sitting in the Pope's chair at the Vatican.

Well, not quite.

Al had brought a bottle of very expensive wine as a birthday gift for Boris. It was a rare Rothschild, probably about a hundred and fifty dollars' worth of cabernet sauvignon, which was a fair bit of change in the seventies. Like it was a baby, Al protected that bottle from being jostled all the way from LA to Copenhagen to the airport near Tel Aviv. When we arrived at the American Colony Hotel in Jerusalem, Al put it down for a moment and the bellman, who was just trying to be helpful, picked it up. Al reached for it and said, "I'll take that!" but the bellman insisted he would take everything and before Al could literally take it out of the man's hands, the inevitable happened and the bottle crashed on the stone floor. The bellman felt terrible, of course, although he surely had no idea that a bottle of wine could be so valuable.

An hour or so later, he showed up at our door with profuse apologies and a bottle of Israeli wine in his hand. The price tag was still on it and it was the equivalent of about twelve US dollars. Later we discovered that at that time in Israel, twelve dollars was about the top of the price list for wine—not exactly what we had in mind as a birthday gift for a special friend. Al rarely got upset about things that were less important than life/death or the loss of a limb, but jet lag and disappointment overtook him and he was one miserable fellow.

By the time we got home, Al had told the story so many times, it was like a stand-up comedy routine. He got a lot of mileage out of it at his Wine and Food Society as members groaned with compassion when he told them what happened to that rare bottle of a fine cabernet.

Boris arranged for us to have a car and driver when we left Masada. I wanted us to stay in a kibbutz, because I found the culture there so fascinating. Someone in the film crew suggested one near the Lebanese border and made a reservation for us. After we traveled for several hours, it was getting dark. Suddenly, I got a sensation in my body that I have had on several occasions, you might call it a physical alert button, which isn't easy to explain.

"We need to change plans," I said. Hearing the anxiety in my own voice and knowing it sounded crazy, I tried to explain the unexplainable. I just knew we shouldn't go there. Nothing had been said or read that related to my anxiety. Al had learned to pay attention to that tone of voice and he didn't argue but the driver was most unhappy because he had plans with a girlfriend at the kibbutz. I insisted, despite his pleading and he took us to Ginosar, which is a kibbutz on the Sea of Galilee where I stayed on my first visit to Israel.

That night, the place where we had originally planned to stay was shelled for the first time. Lebanese rockets destroyed a portion of the kibbutz. I don't know if anyone was killed. I have occasionally, though rarely, had a sense of knowing so strong that I had to honor it and that later proved to be true.

Al often said that I would have been burned at the stake had I lived in earlier times. Probably that was true, but it would have been even more so for my mother or Great-Aunt Mamie.

Mamie (who used to be a jeweler) made an unusually fine living in real estate and said it was because she always knew the kind of houses people really wanted, even when they weren't sure themselves. My mother said if you didn't want Mamie to know something, you should never think about it in her presence.

My mother also had a "gift of knowing" to the extent that she once set the dinner table with an extra plate for her brother, whom she hadn't seen or heard from in a year. Sure enough, without a phone call or a note, he showed up at our door, just about dinnertime.

Years ago, my great-grandmother screamed in her sleep that her son had been killed. At that very hour miles away, he was in a car crash and died. I'm told that she had never done that at any other time.

So I grew up honoring this sixth sense. My husband called me a witch, pronouncing the word very carefully. It would be quite helpful in life if I could summon that sense of certainty when I have doubts about a decision, but I cannot. It comes when it comes, not when I request it. But if I were traveling with my family and about to get on a plane and I had that specific feeling, I would say we must not board the plane. It would be embarrassing and costly, but I would insist we take another flight. I just hope it never happens at the airport. So far, my intuition has served me rather well.

About fifteen years ago, on a whim and a friend's suggestion, I went to see a psychic because a family heirloom was missing that had been passed on from my Great-Aunt Mamie, who died a few years earlier. It was a large diamond in a platinum setting, and I thought it had been stolen. But rumor had it that this woman was extraordinarily good at finding things. My Aunt Winifred once lost her wedding band and a psychic told her to go in the alley and look near the garbage can. She did and there it was, in the dirt. Rather impressive, I thought.

I didn't give Rebecca (not her real name) any information except to say, "Something is missing and perhaps you can help me find it."

Without any hesitation she said, "You mean the ring?"

That could easily have been a good guess.

I said, "Yes, it was a ring."

"It isn't lost; it was stolen." Words came as quickly as if she had witnessed the theft.

"Do you know who took it? Where it is?"

"I don't know his name. But it was in an open container on the dresser where a man's hand reached in and took it! She should have kept her door locked."

"Do you think we could find it in a pawn shop, maybe?

"No, he took it and gave it to another woman."

Now that could have just been a piece of fiction, a convincing story based on a lucky guess. Even so, it confirmed what I thought had happened. I was impressed, but not totally convinced that she was clairvoyant.

A year or so later, Tamara wanted to buy a piece of real estate in Brentwood to build a house. It was in a great neighborhood and was well priced. It seemed like the perfect location for her next building project. But we had some concerns. There was a fault running through part of the property and it would have been challenging to design the house to sit properly on the lot. Another problem was that it was to be sold from an estate and there were many heirs to deal with. These were two very real problems. Ah, but it was a lovely site! I suggested we should go to see Rebecca.

Tamara phrased the situation, "We have a question about a business deal."

Rebecca looked like she wanted some kind of hint. We gave none. She closed her eyes, thought for a moment and then said, "You want to know if you should buy that property?"

Now that's a pretty close hit. We confirmed that, but said nothing more.

Now she took her time. Eyes closed, she put her hands in the air, as if to encompass an image of the land. "Here's the problem," she finally said. "It looks like an underground river runs right down the middle of it. And even without that problem, there are just too many people involved in the deal." She opened her eyes and looked sternly at Tamara. "I wouldn't buy it and I don't think you should either!"

Remember I said that doctors, lawyers and psychics can all be wrong? So now it was our turn to judge what was true. But I doubt you'll be surprised when I tell you we walked away from the deal.

A few years later, I went to see Rebecca again and she

gave me only generic answers to my questions. Nothing useful came of it. I was disappointed and except for those past experiences, I would have felt like I'd paid money to a charlatan. Before I left, I went into her bathroom and I saw many bottles of medicine on the table. I've been told that certain medications can interfere with intuitive insights. If that's true, it may have been the problem that day. Later, I heard that she had cancer.

So now this is the winter of 2008 and I have some important decisions to make. The whole world is rocking from the financial crisis and it isn't only widows who worry about their futures and wonder which experts to trust. (It was 'experts' who got us into this mess, wasn't it?) Remembering the words I wrote today, I'll be especially aware of my vulnerability, acknowledging how even the best of the best can be wrong. The weight is on my shoulders and even though I have excellent advisers, it's my future that lies in the balance of the choices. As the saying goes: *the buck stops here.* I'm grateful for informed consultants who will help me come to my own decisions. I have a fine attorney, a wonderful doctor and I just wish I had an amazing psychic.

Men

There are some things every woman remembers with vivid recollection. Such as, the first time a boy let his hand wander toward forbidden places. For me, the earth-shattering event happened the summer of my twelfth birthday. Everyone I knew liked to dance—yes, even the boys—and summer nights were often filled with friends and rivals who gathered in our backyard where a large and smooth cement area made an almost perfect dance floor. It was a very romantic setting. I had a record player on the porch and we swayed to *Stella by Starlight* or *Body and Soul* or some other music that was popular then.

As I write this, I think about the twelve or thirteen—even fourteen-year-old boys I've seen in the last few years. I can't imagine them loving to slow-dance under an August moon in the heat of summer. I remember dancing on our backyard patio with a gorgeous boy when his heavy breathing was preamble to a rather blatant pass. That cute guy with his wandering hands left me breathless/excited/scared/ and probably a few other adjectives that didn't register at the time. I don't know what I was planning to say or do but I ran in the house and as I whirled around the corner, my father was standing there. He asked me what was wrong.

Anyone who ever wanted to lie to John Baylis Earle would soon realize the futility of the wish. This was not a man you could fool. So I told him what happened and then he taught me a lesson that's been invaluable to me all my life.

"Now, Boots, there's nothing for you to get in a huff

about. He's just bein' a boy. You go back out there and tell him that if he wants to be your friend, he can't treat you like that. No need to seem all upset with him, that'll just confuse him and stir up all kinds of foolishness. You look him in the eye, use a friendly voice, and mean what you say."

That's what I did. So at the age of twelve, I discovered the power a woman has when she shows a clear intention, without a lot of fuss. In later years, variations of that response served me well as an actress in Hollywood. And for the last half decade, when the occasion proved necessary, I would say something like, "I'm flattered, thank you—but I'm married." No need to explain further. It's a good thing to leave a man's ego intact when you can.

A few months ago, a man I met in France was vacationing in California. He came by my office to say hello and I was having a wonderful time, totally fascinated by this charismatic man at least fifteen years younger than I, with twinkling eyes and a beautiful accent. When he was leaving, he pulled me close, then covered my face with a flurry of butterfly kisses. I liked it. Then he *really* kissed me and there wasn't a fiber in my body that didn't remember that I am a passionate woman in the arms of a handsome man. In seconds, I came back to reality, "You're married!" I could hear the frantic sound of my voice as I pulled away from him. So much for sophistication and composure. He looked amused and matter-of-factly said, "Well, yes," in his soft, French-coated voice, just as if I had commented on the blue sky or some other situation totally irrelevant to the moment. Now he pulled me toward him again, holding me close with one hand, going for the gold with the other.

I forgot everything I ever knew about kind rejections. I'm embarrassed to tell you what I said, but in service to honest reporting, I will. I literally pushed him away from me and with no forethought whatsoever I heard myself say, *"Al wouldn't like that!"*

He looked startled, took his hands off my body and

graciously apologized before he quickly headed toward the door, probably appalled by this woman who after all these years on this planet, hadn't learned to just quietly say, "Thank you, but no." When he was gone, I sat alone on the sofa, aware of how aroused I was and how awkwardly I handled the situation. It also made me realize that it was time for me to re-evaluate my life and my plans for the future.

Fast-frame to a week later. I'm having lunch at Stella Mare's restaurant with my daughter and four good friends—three psychiatrists and one psychologist—whom I've known for years. Tamara has a great story-telling talent and she announces to everyone at the table that it's time for me to start dating and she's going to find just the right man for me. "Dad told me to watch out for her and I will. Yesterday I saw this gorgeous man who looked like Sean Connery—and Mom, I know how much you like Sean Connery—anyway, he was in a blue Mercedes convertible and I almost ran into him just so I could meet him and get his phone number!" She shows us her lovely smile.

"That's just great, Tamara," I say. "I'm sure you could read his character in that split-second."

"Mom, you have to start somewhere!" And to the others she says, "At least this one was closer to her age!"

"Tamara, I promised you—I won't date anyone under fifty."

"Sixty Mom, not fifty!"

Everyone at the table is laughing. I'm not sure at which one of us, or probably both. "Well, I have to find someone for her..." She interrupted herself to tell them about our evening together not long ago. "Here Mom was, talking to this forty-something guitar player and he's really working her. She's loving it!"

Now I'm defensive, swearing that I did *not* flirt with that gorgeous guitar player who was telling me how the gypsies originally came from India and how they brought gypsy music to the South of France and all the while he was playing that romantic music...well, he was adorable. But I wasn't flirting. Certainly not.

"I love watching this role reversal!" Karen the psychologist says. Tamara is using that "mother-knows-best" voice and I sound like one of her daughters.

Then Mary says something I can't hear and Zev says, "Tamara, she can go out with anyone she wants to! It's not the age that matters, it's the man! Maybe she's exactly what some young man needs."

Tamara's eyes widen and in a stage-whisper she says, "Zev, any forty-something or fifty-something man who is attracted to my mother is attracted for the wrong reasons!"

At this point I must defend myself and say, "Well I married your first-father for all the *right* reasons and he was twenty-two years older than I was and I deeply loved that man! I wonder if his two daughters thought the same thing about me." I am tormenting Tamara and enjoying every minute of it.

"That was different. It's not so bad when it's the man who is older."

At this point the pro's jump in. Zev accuses her of being sexist, Mary says she was being ageist and Neal stays out of it because he has to leave to see a patient and Karen agrees with Tamara. I think she agrees—we were a rowdy bunch by that time.

Stage-whisper again from Tamara: "I just don't want her to get hurt. She needs someone a little closer to her age." And again my defenders came to my rescue.

"It's her life, Tamara," someone says.

"Well, I promised Dad," she repeated. "If he's younger, he would have to be a very special man."

Zev says, "He'd have to be a very special man anyway, wouldn't he?"

My turn. "This is all hypothetical, you guys. I'm going to stay in Santa Barbara and there are so many more women than men in this town and any man fascinating enough to interest me is probably married or gay! And if he were single and fabulous, he would probably choose a woman in her forties or maybe in her fifties...." And blah, blah, blah.

The poor waiter, who has been hovering, manages to bring the check to our table and we leave the conversation there when we walk outside.

About a year before his passing, Al noticed a man watching me carefully as we walked out of a store. Once outside, Al laughed and said, "Oh Doll, you're going to be so busy after I'm gone!"

He was beginning to let go. But I'm still holding on.

In the last few months of his life, Al said to me, "You can grieve for me a little while when I'm gone and then I want you to get out there and make a good life for yourself. I want you to do whatever makes you happy." He used the same words Mother Picker did, saying what Leonard would have wanted for me, half a century ago.

I need to take a crash course in Dating 101. Or at least practice a little. My skills are terribly rusty. There's a message on my phone from a man I don't know, nor do I recognize his name. A mutual friend gave him my phone number. "I've been hearing about you for years and I just want to get to know you. Would you meet me at Starbucks for a coffee?"

I like that. A coffee takes only as much time as you want it to. It's casual and you can make a quick get-away if things are not going well. If, on the other hand...

"How will we know each other?" I ask when I return his

call and he laughs. "That won't be a problem. I've seen your website."

Of course. So now, I Google him. He's very involved in our community, quite compassionate and generous. An interesting man. My cautious mind takes over and I wonder — is our mutual friend playing matchmaker? (Usually it's women who like to do that.) Is this man calling because he knows about my work and is interested in learning more about 'right-brain' techniques? If that were the reason, he would have come to the office. Did he call because he's interested in a property I might or might not sell? If so, wouldn't he have said so straight away? Is he just interested in my bio that he saw on my website and thinks I might become an interesting platonic friend? Given what I read about him on Google, I doubt he needs another buddy. I decide that I don't have to know. On Monday, I'm going to have a cappuccino with a stranger in a public place. No big deal.

He is waiting for me outside of Starbucks and walks toward me as I come closer. My first impression: handsome, lean, intelligent, gorgeous blue eyes, kind, interesting, maybe in his sixties. All this before he even holds the door open for me. We look for a place to sit. One table is empty and I slip onto the hard wooden chair that has a bench-like seat that wasn't made for the human anatomy. He goes to the counter to order. I wiggle, trying to get comfortable. He brings our drinks, leads the conversation. "So you're a psychologist," he says and I quickly clarify that I'm not. A large portion of my office mail addresses me as 'Dr'. and I'm used to correcting that. Soon he asks me about my husband. Now this response is what I need to work on for future scouting meets. You see, I just start talking about Al and have quite a bit of trouble knowing how much to tell. This man is a patient listener. Totally present. Finally, I ask him about his situation. "I'm happily married," he says.

Oh.

So now I shift perspective, and hope I successfully hide my disappointment. "Well, then, perhaps you and your wife will come to my house for dinner sometime."

I see a reaction. Okay, so he's not trying to expand his social network.

After two hours of nursing our drinks and talking about everything from the economy to spirituality, we walk toward my car. I still don't know why he called me. I sense chemistry but he isn't hitting on me. I'm glad of that because, delightful as he is, I don't go out with married men. We shake hands. He holds mine for a beat longer than usual. "You have pretty eyes." He says.

"So do you," I answer.

And then he says, "If there is ever anything I can do for you, just let me know." And that was the end of that.

Only days later, someone mentioned that a man fitting his description had been asking questions about a property I considered selling. News travels fast in Santa Barbara. There's the local tale that if someone sneezes in the Upper Village, someone in the Lower Village says, "God bless you." Of course, Mr. Charming was digging for information about my building. Wouldn't you think that, at my age, I could spot his intention in a heartbeat?

I guess not. In any case, I decided not to sell the building and I never heard from him or his middle-man again.

Just because I had a terrific dad and two fine husbands doesn't mean that I've become dependent on men. Maybe that just makes it easier for me to trust them. So maybe it's not dependency, just an old habit.

Just an old habit? Ever try to stop eating chocolate or sugar in any form? It's hard enough to break a bad habit, but nothing about my relationship with men has been bad. I like them. The ones who mattered in my life, treated me extremely well; the others were few and long gone anyway.

So here's how a habit starts: you find yourself born in the macho state of Texas in the 1930's and there's an interesting dichotomy: on one hand, men had the political and economic power in the outer world and the authoritative role in the household.

On the other hand, I noticed that my mother always got her own way. And I never heard them argue. Dainty little debutant that she was, she was on a team that built the jigs for bombers at Southern Aircraft in World War II. That required skills in math, engineering and imagination. You talk about "steel magnolias?" Darlin' that is a capital T truth!

I said before, we're from tough pioneer stock. The grandmas on both sides of my family were here during the Revolutionary War, the Civil War, and the War of Texas Independence. They didn't carry rifles but they were soldiers, nonetheless. Someday I'll write their stories. Anyway, I imagine that most of them were pretty tough inside their petticoats and lace. They might have figured out a ladylike way to let their men do the heavy lifting. If they didn't want to mess with something, I'll bet they said it was "a man's job." Not saying that's the way it should be, just sayin' I'll bet that's the way it was.

There's another thing that's worrisome about giving away your power to another person, whether it's a spouse or a teacher or someone whose work you admire. I'm thinking of my "brief encounter" with Irwin Shaw, whose books were drawn to the best-seller list of the New York Times like nails to a magnate.

I met him in the late 1970's when I was a student at the Santa Barbara Writer's Conference. Writers were told to sit anywhere we wanted to at the dinner tables. It just happened that there was an extra chair next to Irwin Shaw, who was a keynote speaker at the conference. So I made a beeline for the chair and, captive audience that he was, he listened patiently as I managed to get the conversation to the novel I was writing. He offered to read a few chapters. He took them back to New York with him, and I didn't expect to ever hear from him but I did. And it was quite a letter. He said, "Here's how I would handle the material," and there were a couple of pages of his suggestions. It was totally different from what I had written, so I wrote him immediately and said, "I'm throwing my novel away and starting over."

By return mail, I got this note from Irwin Shaw, "Wait! What if I'm wrong!"

In all of my years helping writers find their story and their voice, all of my comments hang on the clothesline of that one sentence. My advice to new writers is always to be sure that the advice you are given resonates as valid for you. There's always more than one way to tell a story. Just read a few book reviews and you'll realize how experts may disagree. Listen to criticism with an open mind but don't tear up your writing, or anything you've created, unless the suggestion rings true to you.

I was a student at that conference for two years before Barnaby Conrad invited me to lead a workshop. I met Don Congdon, one of the finest agents in New York and became his client. Before long, I started researching ways to apply the science of hemispheric specialization to creativity in general and to writing in particular. This was the beginning of the program and the book, *The Right-Brain Experience*.

It's strange how that conference, which only lasts one week each June, became my literary home. Every June for the next twenty-nine years, I had the intense joy of teaching classes, being a speaker, helping Mary and Barnaby Conrad choose guest speakers and often introducing them. This is the only place where I met with other writers, shared stories, felt community. That June conference was my New Year's Eve. These were my peeps. This was my tribe. And then in 2006, Mary and Barney sold the conference.

Now we had new management. New management did not understand, like, or intend to continue my right-brain workshop. I was fired. Just got an email saying it was cancelled. I was devastated. It didn't matter that Barnaby said I was one of their most popular workshop leaders; it didn't matter that my history with the conference stretched over decades. Or that my students won awards and plays were produced and books published that began in my workshop. Or that students wrote in protest and some refused to return the following year unless I was reinstated. Nope. Nothing changed the owner's mind.

This terrible feeling of rejection taught me something important about attachment. Why did I allow this one person to affect my happiness to such a degree? It wasn't about money, because she paid a small fraction of my usual fee, it was something much deeper. If I could sum up the message in a line or two of advice to myself and maybe to others, it would be this: Be careful what you become dependent on, attached to, or allow yourself to be defined by, for security is an illusion. It was a valuable lesson, and a painful one. It took a long time for me to get perspective on this.

Then the conference was up for sale again and writer/musician Monte Schulz bought it. In 2014, I decided to reapply and was invited back! So, this year I'll spend my 80th birth-week teaching at the Santa Barbara Writers Conference. That's the best present I could ever have. The trip to Europe I was planning will just have to wait.

A State of Mind

There's a woman in San Francisco who took martial arts very seriously and got her 10th degree Blackbelt in judo when she was ninety-eight years old. And another who still drives herself to work at a hundred and three in Coatesville, Pennsylvania. At eighty and a few years more, there's a woman in Santa Barbara who swims in the ocean every day. My personal desires are not for longevity or an Olympiad's endurance but of a meaningful life with occasional outbursts of joy and a minimum of pain. I'm fascinated by people who do that well. I'll write about a few of them and you'll see that in each of their lives, there is something that denies the common myth that a "real" life ends somewhere before seventy. Popular magazines have a plethora of articles with opinions about what you might want to do in your thirties, forties, fifties, and sixties. And that's that. Don't they know what people in their seventies, eighties, nineties and even in their hundreds are doing? So let me introduce you to some 'seniors' who refuse to wilt like a daisy on a summer day and just go for it. They're living abundant lives for as long as their souls stay in their bodies. I want to write about some of my heroes.

Marge Champion's career as a dancer took off when she was thirteen and Walt Disney hired her to be the model for Snow White in the animated film that is still a favorite with those who love Disney and fantasy. I mentioned her earlier in this book when I wrote about the books we co-authored. She was dancing on Broadway in her early nineties and now, at ninety-five, she is winning awards all over the country for her extraordinary career as a dancer/choreographer in so many venues, including MGM musicals. Marge told me last week that she thinks she's winning all those awards just for living so long. You could expect her to say something like that. It's part of her charm.

In any case, she's living well and joyfully and I have great admiration for the way she's choosing to spend her days, still voting for the Academy Awards, still active as a speaker, still an amazing woman.

Ib Melchior, also ninety-five, and his wife, Cleo Baldon, at eighty-four, are two of the most vibrant people I know. Ib has written twenty-one books, twelve screenplays and produced a countless number of shows for TV and plays for the theater. A new book will come out next December. Cleo is a renowned designer of gardens, houses, furniture, and all things lovely, including her book, "Steps and Stairways." She is still being chosen to design some of the most interesting houses in Beverly Hills and Hollywood. Cleo is probably the best-informed person I know on the subjects of art, history, literature and about any other subject that comes into the conversation. Her first novel *Half-past the Dark of Night* just debuted on Amazon. In a few months, a nonfiction account of her family's migration from Ireland during the potato famine will also be released. *Far From the Land* is a meticulously detailed story, fascinating and literary.

Every year, Ib and Cleo, Al and I, used to meet at a hotel near the beach in Ventura. We would arrive Friday afternoon and leave after brunch on Sunday. Other than eating and sleeping, the only thing we did was critique each other's writing. First, one would read and then the other. Al was the listener. The only thing he wrote was prescriptions but he was amazingly patient with our stories and made valuable comments, which we either incorporated or ignored. Ib honored us both by dedicating his book *Melchior A La Carte* to Cleo, Al and Marilee. We encouraged him to revive stories he wrote that were published many years ago and he has given them new life. If I'm still writing ten or twenty years from now, I hope I have their passion for life and for stories.

Last month they had an intimate little dinner party of about a hundred people at Chateau Marmont to celebrate their 50th wedding anniversary. It was spectacular. They set the bar high and I'm grateful for them.

Ib and I became friends in a rather unusual way and we have different versions of the story. I say I picked him up at a bar. He says no, he's the one who picked me up. (Got your attention there, didn't I?) I was on the hospitality committee at an event hosted by PEN West, an international organization that works for "freedom to write." (It's now called PEN Center USA) Our meeting was at a conference room in the Ambassador Hotel with a bar at one end. I was on the welcoming committee and who walks in the door but a handsome man with the most interesting face and confident demeanor. He looks around for a familiar face. Ah, a newcomer. So, of course, I gave him an official welcome and invited him to sit at my table. "But first, let's get you something to drink." We went straight to the bar. We were old friends before the evening ended and made plans to get together with our spouses. That was only thirty-five years ago.

Dr. Mary Christianson is one of the most important people in my life. I hope I can give to someone else, the loving encouragement she gives to me. She retired from teaching psychiatric residents at Harbor/UCLA Medical Center in her eighties and even in the last few years, has said we should take the stairs instead of the elevator. She knows how to make life work for her at every stage. She also knows how to be a good friend, and stay a good friend through decades of change. We met in the most unusual way:

In 1961, a few months after Leonard died, most people thought I was doing fine. But one dear friend knew my feelings of loss were still wrenching and suggested I "see someone." That was the euphemism in those days for "Get thee to a shrink, Kiddo, you can't just keep faking it!" She sent me to Dr. Bruce Christianson, Mary's husband, and he would not tolerate faking anything, especially that habit I had of crying in the shower so no one knew how much I was hurting. You'll realize how good he was when you remember I married Al thirteen months after Leonard died.

I quit "seeing" Dr. C. shortly after Al and I married. Months later, I heard that he and his wife had adopted twins so I called to tell him I had a gift for the babies. He said I could stop by the house and see his baby boys.

When his wife, Mary, opened the door, she looked like she hadn't slept in days. In the background, I heard the piercing sound of babies screaming in a minor key and not even in harmony. Mary is a child psychiatrist but that doesn't mean she knew what to do with two newborns when she didn't have four arms. She took me to the nursery.

I picked up Jim and she picked up Jeff and somehow between us the boys decided it was time to sleep. Mary and I had a long visit just holding and rocking those tiny baby boys. That was more than fifty years ago and we are still the closest of friends. Jim and Jeff still treat me like their auntie.

Contrary to the usual therapist/ex-patient relationship, the four of us, plus the four children, spent endless hours together and grew into a family. Al and Bruce became close friends and played tennis together once a week. Mary and I have been friends for almost half a century, but only this week we discovered that our family ties tangled a time or two. She is descended from Davy Crockett, I from the Randolph family, cousin of Thomas Jefferson, in whose home young Thomas spent his early years. Both of us had ancestors who fought in the Revolutionary War. (Most of them on the American side.) Both families came to Virginia in the 1600's and moved to Texas before it was a state.

The kicker is this: Among old family papers, I just discovered that it was one of my mother's ancestors who fired the first shot in the Texas War of Independence from Mexico, and it was Mary's ancestor, Davy Crockett, who died in the Alamo during that famous battle. Getting closer, our family ties. Yesterday, Mary called to say that she checked into family albums and discovered that she too, is a descendant of the Randolphs! We've felt like sisters for many years; now we know we're cousins, albeit distant ones.

Great-Aunt Mamie was a hoot. She had a sense of humor that made almost any problem seem minor and when she laughed it was hearty and lengthy besides. Once she started laughing, there wasn't a sour face in the room. It was one of her many gifts. Tall and angular, she had a quiet authority about her. With her auburn hair and intense blue eyes, you would have known she was Irish, even if her accent had more twang than lilt and her family left Ireland to come to Virginia long before the Revolutionary War.

Mamie got a divorce from her husband, Dobbs, in the days women just didn't do that. It was amicable and there were no children. She was an independent career woman with an adventurous past.

Mamie and I had one thing in common; we were treated like adults long before it was time. When one of her teachers in grade school called her mother to say that Mamie had not come to school that day. Her momma said, "Well, if Mamie didn't go to school, I'm sure she had a good reason."

At eighteen, Mamie had no intention of going to college to

be a teacher or to secretarial school, the only options available to a girl without marriage prospects. These were not the careers she was looking for. Her father, who was a jeweler, gave her a sizable diamond ring and she moved to Dallas where she traded the ring for a Packard car. The manager at the car dealership was so impressed with how much she knew about cars, he offered her a job selling Packards. At $5,000 for their most popular model, that would have been the Ferrari of its times. This was in 1913 and I doubt there were many eighteen-year-old woman selling luxury cars in those days. Mamie traded the Packard for the down payment on a duplex and the duplex for an apartment building and the apartment building for a warehouse. Then she went to work for a fine jewelry store until she opened her own office as a watchmaker. When that was a strain on her eyes, she went into real estate. And there she made a small fortune.

Mamie was a great mentor, a risk-taker and enough of a character that she could well be the protagonist of a novel.

She always kept a gun beside her bed and another in the glove compartment of the car. (She lived in Texas, so that explains it.) Thank God, she never used them on a human or an animal but she could do quite well for herself on a shooting range. I had forgotten about the guns when she moved to California and lived in an apartment near our house. One day, I opened her bedside drawer looking for her meds, and there it was: pearl-handled. Delicate. Just as if it meant no harm at all.

Not only was the gun a dangerous idea for any ninety-year-old woman, Mamie suffered from Parkinson's disease and her hands shook, moderately or severely, depending upon her state of mind.

"Mamie, come on! Let me take this thing away!"

"No."

Now I had to be brutal. "Mamie," (This was hard. This was Great-Aunt Mamie, a woman people didn't mess with.) "If a man did break into your room, do you think any burglar worth his salt would be afraid of a ninety-year-old woman holding a little pearl-handled pistol?"

She gave me her most mischievous grin, held her hand in the air as if she were holding the gun and exaggerated her Parkinson's tremor. "He'd run if he saw an old lady doing this!"

She had a point.

Juxtaposed to her free-thinking style was a sense of propriety. When she rented an apartment in Santa Barbara in her eighties, a man got out of the pool and into the elevator without wearing a shirt. She said to my mother, "I'm moving. I won't live around riff-raff!" And in Dallas, she refused to rent her apartment to a Harvard professor on sabbatical because he had a beard! That was back in the 1950's. So there was a side to her I didn't choose to emulate, but when it came to integrity, spirit and courage, she was the best.

Mamie would tell me jokes my parents wouldn't have dreamed of telling. She also told many stories about the family they probably wished I didn't know. "With all those lawyers and doctors and congressmen, you know there had to be some real scalawags in the bunch!"

Mamie died peacefully at our home in Woodland Hills when she was ninety-two but she left a template for a good life in the minds of all of those who knew her well.

Mamie's sister was my grandmother, "Miz Fay," my father called her. She was short and slightly plump and very pretty. Not at all like her sister, Mamie. Moving with a slow Southern molasses style, she did some extraordinary things. When Berlin was isolated from the rest of Germany, creating an island of Western democracy encircled by communists, the only way one could get there was by plane. My grandmother flew over the restricted area to be with her son who was a chaplain in the US Air Force, stationed in Berlin. She used to sneak into East Berlin when it wasn't allowed so she could go to the opera and to buy antiques! My quiet little grandma? It was hard to believe how spunky she was and how much fun.

Years later, when my uncle was stationed near the French/German border and she was living with him, I invited her to visit me in Paris. I had just finished shooting *The Ambassador's Daughter* when she arrived. Sometimes I would come in at 3:00 in the morning or after. (Paris never sleeps, remember?) She would smile and say, "Hi, have a good time?" Now that's the kind of Grandma, I want to be. We would go to flea markets and antique shops and we would laugh like young girls.

When she was ninety-one and in the hospital, I wrote this tribute to her. "Looking backward at ninety, looking forward to heaven, you move from one life-zone to another. You speak of death like it's a vacation you've been promised but never taken; like people you love are waiting there and you're holding up the party; like God himself is fitting you with dancing shoes, feet that won't hurt, and eyes that can see again. Years ago, I remember, 'Grandmother' had too formal a sound, so I gave you love-names and made up songs and stories in your honor. I guess I still do. I'm going to miss you."

When I'm in my eighties and nineties, I hope I can live as creative and constructive life as those I've written about here. And I hope society gets in touch with reality and lets the stereotype of *old people* be replaced by something more vibrant.

Riding the Right-Brain Experience

"Miz Fay" was very much on my mind the first time I went to Berlin. I thought of her sneaking into the communist controlled East Berlin and marveled at her courage and lack of judgment. The Berlin Wall wasn't built in her day, but armed soldiers used to guard the border. She knew how to get around them.

The wall was standing, harshly dividing Berlin, when Al and I drove through Check-Point Charlie twenty-six years ago. That's when I had my first taste of what it was like to be in a communist country. Security was tight. Mirrors were put under the bus we were on, checking for stowaways. I pleaded with Al not to make any of his clever comments that might land us in prison. (Thoughts like that are the downside of having a vivid imagination.) I was thinking of the day before, when we were with a tour at a museum in West Berlin. The guide went on ad infinitum about the devastation the Americans caused to the beautiful city of Berlin. Al's voice shot from the center of the crowd like a sniper's bullet, "Well you started it!" he said. Nobody laughed. The tour guide in East Berlin was saying even more derogatory things about the United States and I held my breath anticipating Al's need to set him straight. It was challenging for him to resist defending democracy, freedom and the American flag, but to my great relief, he managed.

We were in Berlin because I was invited to speak at the *Kongresshalle* on the topic that was central to my new book, *The Right-Brain Experience: an Intimate Program to Free the Powers of Your Imagination*. It was translated into German (and a few other languages) and was released in 1983. Writing that book changed the direction of my career for the next two decades. I originally wrote it for writers but my agent, Don Congdon, said, "It's an important concept. Don't restrict your audience to writers." I changed the book to benefit anyone who wanted to be more visionary, to make more interesting choices for their lives.

Because of the section in the book regarding right and left hemispheres of the brain, I interviewed many brain scientists. But no matter how hard I tried, I couldn't get to see Dr. Roger Sperry, the professor at Cal Tech who was the most highly regarded scientist on that subject. He was a neurophysiologist and neurobiologist and a very busy man. He absolutely refused to give an interview. However, his assistant who taught his classes, Dr. Jay Meyers, was always available to meet with me and eventually to make sure that, in my enthusiasm, I didn't overstate.

In 1981, Dr. Sperry won the Nobel Prize for his contribution to brain research. My book, based greatly on his research came out not long after that. Oh, the timing was so good! Dr. Sperry saw me in a TV interview on "Eye on L.A.," read my book, and said he wanted to meet me. We had several meetings at Cal-Tech and he said some nice things about my work. Then he asked me to co-author a book with him! I was shocked.

"But I'm not a scientist!"

"You don't have to be. I'll tell you what to say."

Oh, those were not the words to win me over, no they were not.

Honored as I was by the invitation, I did not accept.

From this point on, my work wasn't just with writers. I was invited to fascinating places where people from many disciplines wanted to know how to think more creatively. So from Stanford University to a White House think tank, to a fabulous resort in the Caribbean, invitations came faster than I could schedule them and I had fascinating sessions with private clients besides.

In Los Angeles, I received a phone call from a man in Sweden who was president of Pharmecia, the largest pharmaceutical company in the world in the 80's. He asked if he could come to California in two weeks to meet with me. He had read *The Right-Brain Experience* and had heard about my work when he visited Stanford University and spoke with Professor Robert Kim, a man I interviewed in my book. I told him I would love to meet with him but I had a vacation scheduled with my family and we would be in London. "Well then," he said, "May I meet you in London?" And would I please come a day or two earlier than my family so we could possibly do some work before my vacation began?

And so it was, and it was wonderful. Not only did Gunnar Wessman arrange to work with me in Los Angeles in a few months, he asked if I would be available to speak at the World Economic Forum in Davos, Switzerland next January? And would I come to Sweden first to present a short program to the executives of his company?

Watch me in your mind as I try to stay calm and react appropriately to the world's best invitation. The World Economic Forum (formerly the European Management Foundation) is a yearly event for world leaders in business and politics. Two thousand delegates from ninety-one countries come to Davos, Switzerland to hear speakers in various categories of expertise. There are CEO's of international companies, diplomats, Heads of State, and a few Senators. Raymond Barre, former Prime Minister of France was a co-founder of the event. Oh, yes, I think I could work this into my schedule!

Our plans to work together in London were terminated by a phone call from the police: they had just discovered a kidnapping plot on Gunnar's life. In a calm voice, he called me to say he needed to return to Sweden immediately. He would come to Los Angeles in the near future. As it turned out, the potential kidnappers were caught and Gunnar was fine and apparently, not as shaken as I was.

The official invitation for the World Economic Forum came in September and after the first moment of ecstasy, what I felt was anxiety. I, who don't even balance my checkbook, will be a speaker at an economic forum? It took a while to decide how to deal with my rush of delight mixed with terror. I know it's important to live what you teach and so I began using "right-brain" techniques to alter perception. I created this scenario: After a time of meditation, I could feel myself in the conference room. In my imagination, I watched the men enter the room, each of them dropping his business card with his fancy title in a box. Then he would enter the conference room, not as a world leader, but just as an intelligent man wanting to learn what I know how to teach.

This was good. This would work. I expanded it.

I went into more sensory detail. In my mind's eye, I could see the room with dark paneled walls and high ceilings. The box holding the credentials was smooth and made of burled wood. The men who came to the session left their egos and fancy titles with their business cards. They came as curious, intelligent people and the room was almost full. Without using words, I let myself experience the feeling of presentation; I saw the faces in the audience, approving, interested.

As the daydream continued, I imagined some people asking questions and there was a heckler in the crowd who tried to rattle me. Smooth as silk, I was, in my imagination, as I gently and, oh so kindly, listened to his taunting criticism, without defensiveness. I was not unsettled by the man in this imagined experience. From that moment until my presentation, I had no performance anxiety. I repeated the imagery techniques many times until it was seamless, easy, I was on my game. This was fun.

In January, when Al and I stepped off the plane in Switzerland, we did not have to go through customs. A man from the WEF met us, took us around the line to the limousine and up the mountainous road to Davos. The snow was deep and shimmering in the sunshine. For a California girl, it seemed like a fairytale. The clear blue sky had not even a hint of clouds. This was the coldest winter in Europe in many years but it could not have been more beautiful.

The small hotel where we stayed was charming. But when Al and I were coming down the tiny elevator, the doors opened at lobby level and we faced four soldiers with guns at the ready! I gasped and was quickly reassured. They were Greek soldiers, protecting their Prime Minister. "Not to worry, Madam. You are quite safe."

At that time, only men were members of the WEF. Women were welcome to sit in the balcony and not ask questions. Jean Kirkpatrick and I were the only female speakers. (She got the largest room.)

We walked to the conference hall in the crisp air that some thought of as refreshing; to me it was so cold I thought it would freeze my lungs if I didn't warm the air with my gloved hand before breathing it. The sandbag barricade around the entrance, curling right, then left, and right again, came as a surprise. So did the armed soldiers on the roof. But of course, when you have a considerable number of world leaders in one place, you'd better have security. The problem for us was that they were not prepared for a woman wearing a speakers badge or a man wearing one that indicated he was a spouse. Every time we entered, we were delayed as concerned guards called someone who had the authority to let us pass.

When the day came for the first of my presentations, I felt exhilarated and confident. Andrew Young was there from Atlanta and reminded me of our phone conversation a month before. Andrew Young? Oh *that* Andrew Young! I remember getting a call in my office late one afternoon and yes, it was from a man named Andrew Young and we did talk for a very long time about my book but I never thought that it was the former US Ambassador to the U.N and currently, the Mayor of Atlanta! I wish I could tell you I recovered quickly. I did not. It was quite embarrassing and I'm sure he thinks I have early onset Alzheimer's.

I went to the room where my session was held and checked the audio and the lights, the podium and the lectern. Then the room began to fill and I released my earlier embarrassment and allowed the mental programming to take over. There were no wooden panels, but the ceilings were high, the people who came into the room looked not at all confrontational. I relived the story I had created. A warm, relaxed feeling slipped through my body and I felt perfectly at ease. I gave my presentation to a full room, with some men standing at the back. I expected a few aggressive questions, after all, this was a controversial concept about 'right brain' and it would not have been rude if there had been doubters in the crowd. There was not a single hostile critic.

I recognized the author of *Getting to Yes*, Roger Fisher, who was a professor at Harvard Law School and founder of the Harvard Negotiation Project. I thought Senator Bradley was in the back of the room, but I wasn't sure. Then I remembered my mental rehearsal: these men had left their titles when they came in and I stopped thinking of them it terms of their credentials. The speech went well and the audience was the most accepting and enthusiastic group I've ever addressed. Almost all of them were familiar with their own ways to rehearse the future and create the success that they imagined. They asked me back a few years later, when *Inventing the Future* was published. This time, there were many women at the conference, not just spouses, but leaders in important positions. I gave three more presentations and again, the audience was all any speaker could ask for. What an honor and an experience that was.

*****

Perched on the jagged cliffs above the Pacific Ocean in Big Sur, California, the Esalen Institute sits high above a rambunctious ocean with a world famous view. It also has a long reputation of attracting people who are mentally curious and who bring a wide range of spiritual perspectives and adventurous life styles to its famous setting.

My daughter, Tamara and I had just attended a conference on various forms of meditation that lasted several days and we were in that blissful state that comes after hours of stillness and quiet with spiritual intention. We were ready to leave when a woman from India came over to talk with me.

One could hardly miss her among the hundred or so people who attended the meditations for she was stunningly beautiful, wearing a black leotard with no makeup and no jewelry except two enormous diamond studs on her ears. I was not so deep in spiritual thoughts that I didn't notice those earrings.

"You must come to India and stay in our home." She said this about sixty seconds after we met and spoke in a matter-of-fact tone as if the plans were settled.

I laughed, wondering what on earth she was thinking, this woman I had never met before.

"It is meant to be," she said with a tone of quiet authority.

Well, what would you say to that? "That's very kind of you," I replied and quickly changed the subject. She introduced me to her husband but was then distracted by seeing Tamara walking toward us.

"Your daughter is a healer, isn't she?"

I hesitated, then said, "She seems to have a gift." Tamara rarely talks about how her hands get hot when she touches someone who is sick, how the person's pain often diminishes, or disappears. But she is very careful to never overstate. One must be careful about such things. It's important not to raise expectations, or to imply what cannot always be attained.

"Bring your daughter with you when you come. She is welcome in our home."

Another Indian man joined us and when we were introduced, he recognized my name, which doesn't often happen. He told me that when his wife was dying of cancer, she wrote twenty-seven pages of deeply personal feelings based on the instructions in my book, the *Right-Brain Experience: An Intimate Program to Free the Powers of Your Imagination*. Those pages were extremely meaningful to him. He encouraged me to accept the invitation to go to New Delhi, then to travel North to Dharamsala and be part of a small gathering of people who would create an experiential program on Transformational Leadership. There would be no more than a dozen participants and we would work at a retreat house in the Himalayas for five days. Then we would spend time with the Dalai Lama in his home. There was no charge to attend this meeting and no stipends were paid. It wasn't about money.

Of course, I wanted to go, but I said it wasn't possible. My husband wasn't well and should not be left alone for so long. I had deep regrets but it was a clear decision. Although Al was still driving and was pretty self-sufficient, he certainly wasn't a healthy man. But when I told him I refused the invitation, he said, "You call him back right now and tell him you're going! There are plenty of people who will keep an eye on me." Then he gave me that mischievous grin and said, "I'll have parties every night with dancing girls and champagne! Don't you worry about me, Doll."

Right.

I arranged for a friend to stay with Al, then called Dinesh and asked if I could bring my daughter, whose intuitive skills could be quite useful during the sessions. He agreed and I called Tamara. "Do you want to go to India with me?" She didn't miss a beat. "Sure! When do we leave?"

"About two weeks. We have to get a rush order on visas. We'll stay with that nice Indian couple when we're in New

Delhi. Dinesh said they are India's second largest taxpayers so they have a huge house and will even let us use one of their cars and a driver."

When "coincidences" such as our plans for India seem so magical, I pay attention. Let's say that fifty-thousand copies of *The Right-Brain Experience* were sold. (I'm sure it was no more than that, and it might have been slightly less.) Out of the fifty thousand, what is the percentage of terminally ill people who read it? And of the ones who did, how many actually wrote about their experiences based on the suggestions in the book? Then what are the odds that a surviving spouse would be at a retreat center when the one person who was the guide through the 'experiences' was also there? Take it one step further: What are the chances that even if they attended the same conference they would meet? Or that he would remember the author's name after many years and make the connection? What are the odds of all that? Perhaps this trip to India was just…meant to be."

I'm known for being the worrier in the family. After flying from LA to London—with a lovely overnight at the Cliveden Hotel, about half an hour from Heathrow—we took Virgin Atlantic to Delhi. I couldn't help but wonder what we would do if there were no car and driver to meet us. We only had a name, an email address and a phone number. I didn't tell my daughter that such a thought even crossed my mind because she does not appreciate that sort of anxious thinking. When you're really a skilled worrier, it's amazing the scenarios you can come up with. I won't mention them, but if you let your imagination play with trouble, I'm sure you could think of a few yourself.

Of course, the driver was in Delhi waiting for us with our names written on signs and although he spoke not a word of English, he actually showed up! We were not forgotten. He drove us past the hovel of homeless people living under plastic-bag-housing by the side of the road to the great guarded gates of our host's magnificent home. Even before we entered the house, the contrast of great wealth and abject poverty was invading our emotional boundaries. This was our first stay in a private home where men armed with very large guns guarded the gates and patrolled the grounds.

We stepped inside the marble entry and were greeted by our hosts and their children. Then came the news—we must hurry and get dressed for a party! Well, why not? We had only traveled half-way around the world to get there and jet lag shouldn't be a problem unless we allowed it to be. A quick shower, a change into fancy clothes, and off we went.

The publisher of the largest Hindi newspaper in India was having a birthday party and we felt quite excited to see what an Indian bash might look like. It looked like this: High walls around a gorgeous house. Several guards. Big guns. Wonderful exotic music. Fantastic food. Diamonds and rubies and emeralds everywhere, huge stones on fingers and ears and noses. Silk saris. Smart and charming English speaking guests. It was fabulous! Then...

The conversation turned to the morning paper, which carried an article that was creating a great deal of excitement because it named names and revealed abuses and it had made some very important people extremely angry. Also, there was a throw-away line that someone just happened to mention: The publisher's father, and before that his grandfather, had both been assassinated because of political articles they published in that paper. There was concern about the safety of the host.

There was absolutely nothing Tamara and I could do. Just drink something cold, eat something hot, smile and dance and know that life is short and things happen. Hopefully, not tonight.

We had a few days to see Delhi before taking the train to Dharamsala. During that time, Tamara did several healing sessions, which were very effective, and I did some pro-bono consulting. We were having a great time with our hosts and their friends, but both of us had trouble reconciling the abundant luxuries of our stay with the devastating poverty outside its walls. We didn't see anything as wrenching as the scenes in *Slumdog Millionaire* but my daughter and I have porous boundaries when it comes to seeing so many people in need.

It was cool in Dharamsala, in the foothills of the Himalayas. From the retreat house, Tamara and I drove with eight others down the narrow mountain road in Northern India, past the tents of venders, past the refugees who were given asylum from the Chinese. We passed through a security check and waited in a reception room at the home of the Dalai Lama. There were about ten of us, and this was the final day of the Transformational Seminar that was held only a mile away. Tamara said, "Mom, I never get nervous about meeting anybody, but I'm nervous now!"

I would have felt the same at her age but at this point in my life, I don't put anyone on a pedestal. He is undoubtedly an exceptionally fine man, but he's flesh and blood like the rest of us. He may be wiser and smarter, but he's still just a guy.

Swathed in his crimson robe, the Dalai Lama entered the room. We stood, and each of us walked past him to be introduced. I had expected him to greet us like all our Indian friends have done, with hands clasped palm to palm beneath his chin. It surprised me when he extended his hand, and when I took it, he used his other hand to complete the exchange. I certainly never expected a charge of hot energy to fly from his hands, up my arm and through my body! I don't put people on pedestals, remember? But perhaps just this once, it's okay. When that man made eye contact with me, I felt like there wasn't a secret in my life he didn't know.

We sat in a circle of straight-back chairs and listened as he spoke to us for a few minutes—I can't remember one single thing he said, which seems strange. But I tell you truly, the Dalai Lama has an energy that you can feel from across the room. When it was time to ask him a question, I knew the one that was heavy on my heart and I said, "It's one thing to forgive someone who hurts you, but how do you forgive someone who hurts someone you love?"

He looked at me in silence, brown eyes piecing, strong and gentle at the same moment. He didn't speak through his translator when he answered me and he took his time. It seemed as if he were letting the words come to him as a new thought, as if he were rethinking his answer—which you and I both know couldn't be the case—just consider how he must have struggled to answer that same question for himself, considering the Chinese atrocities in his homeland of Tibet.

Finally he said, "When someone has hurt a person you love, you may hate the act itself, but the one who did the harm is your brother or your sister and must be forgiven."

I felt like I had failed Buddhism 101. (Christianity, too, for both share that same message.) Before our time was over, when our picture was taken with His Holiness and we were given a silk prayer scarf as a memento, I left with a feeling of reverence, and the decision that just maybe, it was all right to allow just one pedestal in my life.

We drove down the winding road to the train station, to Delhi, to London, to LA and home again to Santa Barbara.

One Fine Day

The phone rings and it's Sidney Picker, my nephew via Leonard. "There's going to be a family reunion and we want you to come." Sidney, oh my goodness! What a lovely man he is and I hear the familiar East-Coast-Picker sound in my ear. I'm overcome by a flood of memories. Yes! Of course I'll be there. It's been too long since I felt the warmth of their hugs.

"Tell me when and where."

He does, and of course, adds, "Gina and Tamara too, and all of their children?"

How wonderful is that. Sidney is an international lawyer who has a dry intellectual wit that is a Picker trait. He's a great storyteller and I miss him.

Mother Picker got the family together on her birthday numerous times but that was long ago. Reunions used to be at the Plaza Hotel in New York. This time, Sidney chose a casual resort in Maine. No fancy clothes, sort of a *come as you are* gathering which turned out to be about seventy people.

I rented an old farmhouse near the lake for the week. Tamara, Jeff, Madison, Mckenna and I flew from Santa Barbara, Gina and her husband, Greg from Phoenix. Gina's three grown children were stuck with jobs they couldn't leave. Ashleigh couldn't get the time off from the hospital. Taylor had just started a new job with a Reality company in Palm Springs, and Cameron was holding his breath for an interview he couldn't risk missing.

The road to the party wandered through gentle hills and under the branches of sprawling oak trees, past a lake straight out of a Norman Rockwell painting. The family had already started to gather and Jeannie Firstenberg was the first one I saw. She's the epitome of cool. One must be extraordinarily confident to seem so powerful, just standing there. Jeannie is my niece and has done a great job as President of the American Film Institute. She's low key and earthy and seeing her here makes me wish we had spent more time together over the years. We hug, and in the process I spill only a little chardonnay down her back. She laughs. I cringe.

I catch my breath when I see Sue Ann and Rae Ceil. Leonard's daughters from his first marriage. They are beautiful as ever and we fumble through superficial chatter until we really get down to talking about their father and the things that happened long ago. Tamara has never met her half-sisters. When Leonard and I married, the older girls pulled away. I think that was a loss for all of us.

Gina remembers once she was with Al at a Wine and Food Society dinner at the Beverly Hilton, when I was out of town. In the lobby, she said to Al, "That girl looks like me." Indeed she did, for it was Sue Ann. That was the only time they had met since Gina was three years old.

It is a tender meeting at the reunion and the sisters and half-sisters take full advantage of this time together. I think it is meaningful for all of them. I know it is for me.

Then I see David Picker, my nephew, Jeannie's brother. He's three years older than I am. Do his eyes really fill with tears when we hug? Did I imagine it? I feel closer to him this moment than I ever have. It used to be that I felt shy with him, I don't know why. I was accustomed to being with powerful men, but David was one of Hollywood's most successful producers and studio executives. He was President and Chief Executive Officer for United Artists, Paramount, Lorimar, and Columbia Pictures. He produced more than thirty films, most of them you've seen, if you're as hooked on movies as most of us are. I'm remembering a few of the actors: Dustin Hoffman, Sean Connery, Daniel Day-Lewis, Steve Martin and the Beatles. And that's just for starters. David is an

Oscar, Emmy, and golden Globe nominated producer. You may remember some of his favorite films: *Tom Jones*, the *James Bond* series, a *Hard Day's Night*, *Midnight Cowboy*, *Last Tango in Paris*, *Lenny*, *The Crucible*, *The Jerk*. And on and on.

Despite the genius and the accolades, the man I'm holding and spend hours talking with is not the powerful executive to me; he is the gentle, beloved son of Eugene, Leonard's oldest brother, who was always so kind to me when times were hard. At dinner we sit together and he tells me how much Mother Picker loved me and I, who have a tendency to deflect kind words, said, "I know she adored Al."

David looked at me with such intensity when he said, "She loved you, Marilee. And she gave the cross on the top of the church in Leonard's name. That was big."

Yes it was. And that probably needs some explaining.

When Leonard and I were dating, he invited me to Sunday brunch at a friend's house. I said I liked to go to church on Sundays. He said, "Okay, I'll go with you. We can go to the party after that."

He came with me several Sundays, and scholar that he was, he started doing his own research into Scripture. Then he said, "Can we go to some other church, next Sunday? Does it have to be Methodist?"

I was amused. "No Leonard, it doesn't have to be Methodist. It can be any church that doesn't have closed communion."

"What's that?"

"That means you have to be a member of that church to take communion. I don't believe there are any lodge seats in heaven."

He was quite befuddled. Soon after, United Artists had a party for the opening of "Fuzzy Pink Nightgown," starring Jane Russell, who was well known not only for her physical attributes but for her Christian commitment.

I was talking to someone else but Leonard and Jane's conversation caught my ear. Jane said, "If you really want to know what Christianity is, you have to meet Lou and Colleen Evans. They just started a church in Bel Air and meet in a public school on Sundays."

"A church can't meet at a school!" said my Constitutionally-minded husband.

"Well, this one does."

I think the first reason we went there was because he wanted to see if that was really true. Church and Government? A separate thing in his mind.

The following Sunday we were there, in the auditorium of a grammar school. I'm sure I've never been in a room that radiated such warmth and acceptance. I know Leonard was touched by it. There was something happening there that fascinated him. Although Leonard hadn't practiced Judaism since his bar mitzvah, he took great pride in being a Jew. Even so, something about the message and the people moved him deeply. Every Sunday, we attended services and he started taking classes. Several months later he said, "I do feel the presence of Spirit, here. Now I understand what you meant. And I want to be part of this."

Within a year he was a member, then an Elder, a member of Session (think Board of Directors). He lectured to large audiences in that powerful, tender voice he had. He was radiant. Sometimes I felt like I had married an apostle. His enthusiasm could be overwhelming.

When he went to Germany to speak at a conference, I didn't want him to go. I was pregnant and had a premonition that it was dangerous for him to be there. I argued against it. I lost. But he promised he wouldn't cross into East Berlin, which was in Communist territory, and it was the middle of the Cold War. At least that was one worry I didn't have.

Then I got a phone call from Berlin. Leonard said he had to take back that promise; he wouldn't go without telling me, but he couldn't tell me why until he returned. There was no point in arguing.

When he came home, I heard that he brought medicine

into East Berlin and that he preached there. He helped a young boy escape to the West. He was on top of the world. And that was in the fall of 1960. Only a couple of months before Tamara was born. Was he really in danger there? Yes, he was. The story could easily have had a different ending.

It had been devastatingly hard for Leonard to tell his family about his faith, and to let them know that his decision did not take him from Judaism; it led him back to his heritage in a profound way. He would always be proud of that. When he died and his mother came to his service that was in our new church high on a hill overlooking the Valley, she turned to me and in the sweetest voice said, "I could find my peace here." She knew Leonard had wanted to donate a cross that would go on top of the chapel when it was finished. Now, she said she would like to be the one to do that.

If Leonard had lived longer, he would have written about the spiritual journey that had such meaning in his life. At first, it wasn't easy for his family to understand the spiritual path his life was taking but they told me many times that they had never seen him so happy. He embraced the loving compassion of both faiths and denounced the intolerance that can sometimes appear in each of them.

So many people at the Picker celebration had fascinating lives and made great contributions in the film industry. And I'm thinking about those who are no longer with us: the four brothers, Leonard, Arnold, Eugene, Sidney. Each left their footprint in the history of film. The most amazing story of all is that of Leonard's father, David V. Picker. He came to the United States from Russia, entering through Texas, instead of Ellis Island. He made his way to New York and went into the clothing business. When unions made it impossible for him to make a profit, he went into bankruptcy. He wasn't down for long and a few years later, he built his own theater chain, then joined Lowe's in the theater business and in time made a fortune. He held a party at the Waldorf Astoria for all the people who lost money as a result of his financial troubles, then repaid them with interest. If the benefactor had died, he repaid their families. This is the code of honor that's rooted in the souls of this remarkable family.

I love them more than they know and will never forget the emotional generosity they showed to me. When I stood to say that at the party, to thank them all, the excitement of the evening, or the extra glass of wine at the table tangled my words. I'm not sure, even then, that I was able to say how deeply blessed I have been by their thoughtfulness. How many memories were stirred by those days with Leonard's family? How many stars are in the sky?

Before Al had his last surgery that sent him in a downward spiral, I dreamed of Leonard for the first time in many years. In the dream Leonard said, "Ask Al if I can be the one to meet him when his time comes and I can bring him into the light."

I told Al about the dream.

"That would be wonderful, Doll." His eyes misted. "I would like that."

That night I meditated for a long time and then held Al's answer to Leonard's question in my thoughts—"Yes, Al wants you with him when he passes." I wish I could say I had some sensation of knowing that this message was received, but I did not. I tell you only what I know to be true: I had a dream. In the dream, Leonard stated his wishes. Al accepted. I was just the messenger. How that works, I have no idea. Nor does anyone, no matter what they tell you.

*****

I've always thought there was some inexplicable connection between Leonard and Al. There is no logical way to explain what happened one morning more than fifty years ago. Leonard woke up and said he had a disturbing dream that someone died. My analytical, lawyer husband had never shown interest in telepathy or the interpretation of dreams but he was obviously concerned. That made no sense at all. And the next thing he did, didn't make sense either. He called our minister, Lou Evans and asked him if there had been a death in the congregation. And the answer was yes. To be accurate, it was the *father* of someone in the congregation. It was the father of one of Leonard's friends: Frank Zdenek. The man who would be my brother-in-law in a few years.

So long before I met Al, Leonard went to the funeral of his father. I had a baby to care for so I didn't go. That night Leonard told me about the funeral and how hard it was on Frank's brother, who grieved so deeply for his dad. "I like that doctor," Leonard said, "He's a good man."

There was another time they met, as well. Leonard held a screening for the Brazilian movie, "Black Orpheus." I had been up most of the night with the baby and was exhausted. I stayed home. Leonard often invited friends to screenings and this time he invited Frank, who—you have probably already guessed—brought his brother. I remember Leonard saying again, how much he liked Al.

I have always believed that, in some inexplicable way, Leonard chose Al to be with me when he was gone, to help me raise those beautiful baby girls.

A few months after Al's passing, when I was feeling so terribly lonely, I meditated and told Al, "I just can't do this alone." At that moment, I felt the energy of Al and Leonard both, like old buds, in the room with me. I felt their love and comfort. The intensity of that moment passed, but it left me sure of one thing—I am only as alone as I think I am.

If anyone ever tells you that you can't love two men at the same time, remember this story. I will always love these two men. I will be eternally grateful for having them in my life.

Flames in the Hills

It is almost sunset when a friend yells, "Look out your front door!" Neighbors are gathering outside my house, all looking in one direction, considering the odds, accessing the direction of the winds. This is California; we know about fires.

I try to gage the distance between the flames and my home. I'd say about five miles, maybe less. Someone says, "The wind's not blowing this way. I think we'll be fine." As if the wind can't change its mind.

I start thinking about what to take, if the time comes. The smoke spreads across the distant hills. Houses are burning. Helicopters fly overhead. Fire trucks wail in the distance.

"I'm packing up," I say. Remembering.

The first things I think about are the photographs and how glad I am that I have copies of every one of them at the office. Losing my pictures would hurt more than losing everything else in the house.

Flames claw their way toward the sky and when it's dark it's hard to tell how far away the fire is. The smell of smoke permeates the air. A couple of years ago, I bought an SUV because Al's wheelchair would fit in the back. Now I'm glad I have the room for so many things. It's ten months to the day, when Al's Spirit left this earth. Fires and death seem fused in my associations and I try not to remember how it was the first time, so long ago.

I pack my photographs, my manuscripts, then the smaller paintings, wrapped in towels. Then some sculpture, the ones I can carry, and things that were safe in my Great-Aunt Mamie's house when the Bel Air fire came, years ago. I choose my mother's drawings and a small toy I had when I was a baby that was in my Grandmother's attic when Bel Air burned. And of course, my laptop and iPhone. Everything I can carry that I'll need if the fire claims my house. Everything I love that is here that I can lift. I watch the direction of the flames each time I take a new load of my favorite things out the door.

"Ortega Ridge is burning," someone says, and that's the next hill over. "It's not Ortega," a woman says. "It's not that close." Maybe not. But once burned — as the saying goes.

Memories race into the present, pushing reason aside, dragging all the old panic and vulnerability that overwhelmed me half a century ago. My hands tremble. The past co-exists with this moment and I feel terribly alone.

I go into each room of my house and mentally say a ceremonial goodbye to all the things that have made my life so beautiful and are too heavy for me to lift or too fragile to carry. Each item is a reminder of the person who gave it to me, or the experience that brought it into my life. There's a cattail curve on the arms of a mahogany chair that belonged to my great-grandmother, I have a picture of her sitting in that very chair in the 1800's. The glass candlesticks Al bought for me in France years ago that remind me of the lavender in Provence — and of him. They might survive the fire but probably not the twisting road down to the freeway. "I hope you're here when I get back," I say aloud to my things. My children will tell you that sometimes, I'm a bit peculiar. I am trying very hard to stay calm. I am my mother's daughter, after all. That should have put some courage in my DNA.

Driving slowly down the narrow road toward the freeway, I think about the last time I ran from flames. This is different, I tell myself. The only thing the fire can take from me this time is my home and my belongings. Even so, I am fearful.

I wish I could tell you that I live with my roots in my pocket, unencumbered and free. But that's not who I am. I'm one who is grounded to the land, to *my* land. To my home. To every memory linked to everything inside it. I realize that the things I think I own, seem to own me.

Where will I go now, tonight? Everyone I know well enough to call for help is equally in danger. I drive to my office where I might spend the night and am told that the building has to be evacuated. I turn toward LA, but feel too tired to make the trip and although I want to be safe, I don't want to be too far away. Besides, I'm low on gas and just too weary to even fill the tank. I turn off in Carpentaria and drive to the Best Western Hotel where the parking lot is lit and packed with evacuees. I don't dare leave my car, given the possessions I rescued. The seat of the car will lean way back and I thought to bring a pillow and a blanket. I could do with a glass of wine but—oh, well. I'll be perfectly safe for the night. I no longer feel anxious, just depleted. Even the intensity of my fear has dissipated and numbness has taken over.

My cell phone rings, again, again, again. It's Gina, calling from Phoenix, then Tamara calling from France and Sheri from North Ranch, Cleo from Hollywood, Zev and Neal from Montecito, Paul from the mountain high above my house, people I love from everywhere, offering their homes, giving advice. I feel comforted by their concern.

"Mom! Are you out of your mind?" Gina is indignant. "You are a seventy-five year old woman and you cannot sleep in your car in the parking lot of the Best Western! *What are you thinking!*"

"I'm thinking that I can't leave my car in a parking lot with all my favorite things inside. How 'bout that?" I try to sound lighthearted. I manage a laugh, but it has a theatrical sound to it. All those acting lessons from years ago kick in and I start faking what I feel. It's like riding a bike. You never forget.

Oh, I get such a lecture. But Gina is miles away and the power is mine. "I'm staying."

"Well, you should at least go to the Four Seasons."

"Thank you, Gina; I can just see it now: I'll drive up to valet parking at the Four Seasons and ask the attendant to park me in a very safe place because I'll be spending the night in my car. I'm sure they'll welcome me with open arms."

Eventually, Gina wins and I agree to go somewhere else. I don't know where. My friend, Paul, calls to say that he can't see any flames now—his house is higher in the mountains than my own, he certainly would know if there were still a threat. He says it looks safe but if I don't want to be alone, I can come there and sleep at his next-door neighbor's house; his own home is already filled with evacuees. I'm comforted by the thoughtfulness but I am just too weary to meet people I don't know, or even to talk to those I do. Fear of loss is hard on the body. Moods are mercurial: one minute I'm trembling, the next I'm sarcastic, most of all I'm just so very tired.

I'm thinking about our little cottage and remembering the day we saw it for the first time. The broker didn't have a key to get in but when I saw Al's face, like a little boy on Christmas morning, looking at that incredible expanse of ocean and the islands in the distance, I knew it was long past time for me to get over my fear of living in the mountains. I knew what he was thinking and I said, "We'll take it." Al grinned but the broker looked shocked, "Don't you want to see inside! I can get a key in the morning."

I said, "No. Whatever's wrong, we'll fix it."

And so we did. I turned it into a playhouse. Walls are now dressed in vibrant colors and a sari swings from the low ceiling in the entry, disguising the lack of height. An inlaid French dining table seems right at home next to a carved Balinese sideboard. Modern art hangs an arm's length from my great-grandmother's cattail chairs from the mid-eighteen hundreds. We added a living room but that only brought the house size up to all of fifteen hundred square feet. I insisted on adding a walk in closet. I would share anything in my life with Al except a clothes closet.

It's interesting how many people who have grand estates rave about our tiny nest. Perhaps they sense the freedom that comes with rebelling against the expected.

Feeling as though I'm moving through a dream, I drive back up the mountain and realize that I can see my home, still standing, and the flames far in the distance. I leave my car packed, facing the street with my treasures locked inside. Neighbors are watching the hills through the night, just in case, and will call me if the winds shift. I trust them. I leave my shoes at the door, drop my sweater over a chair and climb into bed, clothes and all. I don't wake even once during the night.

The next morning, the fire is subdued by the courage of firefighters and the quieting of winds. Still, I wait to unload my car. I've learned to be cautious.

I take my coffee to the patio, with a rag to wipe the ashes off the table and a chair. The ocean is a strange titanium color and I can't see the islands for the heaviness in the air.

Why do I want to live here? Where fires rage through the hills as if on schedule and you never know when it's time to pack up.

There are safer places to live. Of course there are. Then I remember the story (which may be apocryphal) of a community of people who fled the earthquake of Northern California for the safer land in Kansas. There are no earthquakes in Kansas. There are, however, tornados. Lots of them. And one year, all those people who ran from the earthquakes of California were killed by a tornado in Kansas when the winds tossed cars and people and houses toward the sky.

I consider the hurricanes in Florida, the floods in Ohio, the freezing weather in Maine, the tsunami's in Thailand and Japan, and on and on the story goes. Running away isn't the answer. So what is the answer? I asked myself. How do I take care of myself in a world where there is no such thing as security?

Like Scarlett O'Hara, I decide to worry about that tomorrow.

An Elixir for Bad Dreams

Carl Jung said, "Dreams are letters from the unconscious and we should start opening our mail." I wake from an unfriendly dream and don't need a PhD to interpret the meaning. I've read this letter before and I get the message. It's perfectly obvious why I feel so lonely in this bed that's made for two with just me in it. I think that packing up for the fires by myself, choosing what may be all that remains of my personal treasures, really hit me hard. I search for memories that comfort me, random thoughts that are remedies for depression. This usually brings me to thoughts of children.

When your children have children, you are defined forever more as a grandmother. When a dear friend and Arts Editor of the Los Angeles Times, Charles Champlin, introduced me for a speech I gave at the Santa Barbara Writers' Conference; he made this fabulous introduction and then ended it with "...and can you believe she's a grandmother?"

At that time, I was not ready for that word to be part of my professional identity! No one in my family used that term. Not for the four generations I know about, anyway. It made me think of little old ladies with white hair in buns, bony elbows and canes.

There's nothing wrong with white hair, boney elbows and certainly not with canes. It's just that I was not ready for that as a public image. Or a self-image either. It was the stereotype of the frail grandmother I resisted, not the relationship. My children called their grandmother Nanoo. I called my

Grandmother, Mom (and my mother I called Momma.) Momma called her grandmother Bammaw. I heard about a party a woman gave and she asked all of her guests to bring suggestions for what she should be called when her daughter's first child was born. She said the winner was: "Your Royal Highness."

I decided to let my first grandchild decide what she would call me. The name Ashleigh coined was Boga. With a soft "o." Now five grandchildren, their parents and their friends prefer that name for me. Oh well. It's a love name.

In my mind's eye, time rolls backward and I see Ashleigh watching a French film on TV with great concentration. I have no idea why she is so fascinated; this little five-year-old can't possibly understand the language or the story. I sit beside her. She is transfixed and I wait to see what she'll say about this movie that's in a language she doesn't understand. "What's the movie about?" I ask her. What she tells me has nothing to do with the actual film that has so completely engrossed her but she doesn't hesitate to tell me the plot. She reports an adventure with a beginning, middle and end—and it's a pretty good story. Now, I am fascinated. Do we have another writer in the family? There's a momentary flashback of reading my stories to my mother and my grandmother. A déjà vu with different casting. Ashleigh dictates her stories to me on a regular bases. I save them all.

Time passes and then this lovely child is all legs and long blonde hair, blue eyes and she's maybe eight? Nine? She plops herself down in my lap as I sit in a comfy chair and I see the look of dismay on her face. She looks at me with deep sincerity and sadly she says: "Boga, I don't fit anymore." I have to accept the fact that all too soon she will be a teen and things will change. I tell her that I don't care if we fit in the chair—she will always fit in my heart.

A quiet peacefulness invades my mood and the sadness wanes.

I'm thinking of another little girl with the golden-brown

eyes of a mystic who used to bring a pillow and blanket to the floor beside my bed in the middle of the night. She was seven, maybe eight. Taylor would make a nest for herself where she could see the moon and whisper, "You, sleepin' Boga?"

I would drop my arm over the side of the bed and stroke her arm. "I'm awake, Sweet Pea." And then she would tell me what she dreamed about, or worried about, or anything that weighed heavily on her mind.

"Do I have to stop reading *The Purple Pelican*?" she whispered one night, not wanting to wake Al.

"Of course not. Why would you?" I whisper back.

"My teacher said I read at a fifth grade level so does that mean I have to read big girl books instead of the ones I like?"

I slip down beside her on the blanket. She tosses her long, dark hair over the pillow and we both watch the moon through the large glass door and I say all the things that grandmothers say at times like this. "How about we read it together, because I haven't outgrown *The Purple Pelican* either. A day will come when you'll ask me to save this book for you in your box of special things that you can keep forever. But I don't think either of us is ready for that now."

It is a magical time we share, and I wonder what this beautiful right-brained child will do with her rich imagination and artistic skills. The world will open its arms to her, I think. She, whose dimples and dark, expressive eyes remind me so much of her beautiful mother, Gina, and of Leonard.

This is a memory that brings me pleasure, and it's as fresh as if it happened only yesterday—and again tonight, right now, as I relive it in my mind. Memory is powerful. It can pull you out of a slump or push you deeper into one. It's a choice.

I remember a heat wave in Paris a few years ago and pull it from my repertoire of favorite moments. Our vacation is near its end and some of the family have already flown home. Al is in a wheelchair now, and trooper that he is, he has never complained about the heat or the fact that cobblestones are pretty hard on both the rims of wheelchairs and the derrière of the passenger. I'm grateful for the handsome young man who pushes his grandpa over the jagged streets of the Left Bank with such devotion. He loves Al so much he will do anything to make his ride more comfortable.

We decide to take a boat ride on the Seine early in the evening and watch the lights turn on in the city. There is such joy in watching the two of them. I hold my breath when Cameron clutches the handles of Al's chair, carefully maneuvering him down the long steep ramp to the water. It takes others to help get him in the boat. And then we feel the evening breeze in our faces and the damp air of the Seine cools our skin. It is my favorite experience in Paris—except for Musee d'Orsey, except for Saint Chappelle, except for...maybe I shouldn't even use the word *favorite* in this city. In any case, I'm grateful for this boy/man who is so adoring, who knows—must know—that there will not be many more trips with his beloved Poppy.

When it was time to share some of Al's things with those who loved him, Cameron only wanted a pair of Al's shoes. It would be a long time before his feet were big enough to wear them, but he treasured them. Along with Al's Captain's cap from his service in World War II.

And then there is our Drama Queen. The powerful Miss M. McKenna Nicole Riley. She rides her new tricycle on the sidewalk, veering off until *wham*, she hits a tree and with the rage only a queen could muster, she looks at the tree and says, "Excuse me! I was riding my bike here!"

Oh, sweet McKenna, if that tree had known how to do it, surely it would have picked up its roots and relocated. As you grow older, I think you'll move mountains, or at least bushes or maybe you'll just grow a soft pink-tinted voice, ask a tree to step aside, and it will be done. But now we are in the real world; you are eighteen and instead of going to your high school graduation party, you take a plane to Thailand by yourself to volunteer in an orphanage in Chiang Mai and then to an elephant sanctuary where I see a photo of you washing an elephant in the river. I wrap the memory around me like a hug from the past.

There's another Miss M., the reserved one with the softest voice, the most observing eye, and the one who is the most adventurous of all. We take Madi to the Caribbean when she is ten weeks old, to France and Austria when she is still in diapers and with a bottle.

In Vienna, Mozart's opera "The Magic Flute" is performed with marionettes. It's popular with tourists and since it involves puppets, we assume it's for children. Since Madi is so well behaved, we take her to the theater. To our surprise, the theater is filled with adults and only a sprinkling of older children. We know we can rely on this little seasoned traveler to listen to the music for a moment, cuddle with her fuzzy white bear and sleep through this evening performance.

She is quiet as the proverbial mouse, but sleep is not in her plan. Madi smiles as the music pleases her, she doesn't miss a thing that is happening on stage. All goes well until one of the puppets whacks the other one with a stick. "No! No!" yells a frantic little soprano voice, its timber swelling in volume, rising above the music. We make a quick get-away, avoiding eye contact with those who are seated on the aisle.

I wonder the part this early exposure to travel set her up for the life she's chosen. And I wonder if someday she'll relive her stories about studying in Spain and Italy, Argentina and Chile with her Bachelor degree from The American University in Paris and her Masters degree from King's Collage in London. How will she remember these early adventures when she's my age?

As I lie in my bed and reliving these stories, imagining what their lives will be, the nightmare is forgotten and I'm relaxing in gratitude, comforted by the love in this family, soothed by memories. Suddenly, it is morning. In gratitude, I wake to a beautiful day.

What Really Matters

Timing is everything and what better time than now to get a phone call from a very special friend with a great idea. There's a time to receive and a time to give back. Margi Mainquist had the right words at the right moment in my life.

"Would you like to serve on the Board of Directors at Hospice of Santa Barbara?"

HSB is a non-profit organization that helps those who are dealing with a terminal illness, who don't want to die in a hospital, who need comforting or advice. They offer counseling for the families; therapists and volunteers go to the homes of those who need end of life care; they help children in the schools who have lost a grandparent or a parent or a friend. They never charge for their services and never turn anyone away. Because they take no government money, they are obligated only to the values of the organization. HSB exists because of the generosity of the community.

"If the Board wants me, I'm honored to be part of it."

All board members also serve as volunteers in an area of their expertise. My first presentation was to give a series of three workshops using guided imagery to help people deal with grief. The first session was for the caregivers, who sometimes forget to take care of themselves while doing such intense work with loss. Then different imagery was presented to comfort the loved ones and finally, gentle and positive imagery was suggested to make an easier passage for those whose life on earth is ending.

Sometimes I've presented short sessions for the community at the HSB building and recently I joined, Mary

Wagner, a Marriage and Family Therapist, in offering a program titled, "Who are You, Now?" So many who find themselves alone, after many years with a partner, need help in redefining who they really are. Like Alice, in her Adventures in Wonderland said, "I can't go back to yesterday because I was a different person then." Lewis Carroll wasn't thinking about widows when he wrote that but the words still apply. Living in yesterday doesn't help one to survive and invent a meaningful life for the present. Yesterday isn't there anymore. But memories from the past can be used to shed a light on the possible future. Acknowledging that we are not the same after the loss of a husband or wife, is a preamble to healing.

I'm so glad Margi recommended me to the Board. I've known her for more than twenty years and we've shared both good times and hard. She went through the stages of grief shortly before I did. It's good to be working with her again, not just presenting seminars, but serving at Hospice of Santa Barbara.

Again, Again, Again

It is the early afternoon on the 5th of May, 2009. In downtown Santa Barbara, I'm having a CAT scan for a problem that turns out to be nothing of consequence. Waiting for the technician, I look out the window and see flames in the hills not too close—but not too far away either. Not again! I'm thinking. "How long will this take," I ask about the procedure, knowing I'm half-an-hour from home if there's no traffic and I don't know how far or how fast the flames are spreading.

When I walk outside into the smoke-filled air, I realize there's more than one fire, for the sky is turning crimson at both ends of Santa Barbara and the wind is definitely in control of the city's future.

When I get home and assess the fire, I know that it's time to pack up my car. Again. It's only been nineteen months since the last time! And forty-seven years since the one that changed my life forever.

I pack the same things in the same way but this time I'm strangely calm. I hurry, but there's no panic in the process. I triage the valuables, plucking the most-loved and the most-needed.

Tamara and Jeff are back from living in France, Madison and McKenna too, of course. They live in Hope Ranch, at the other end of Santa Barbara. Tamara is packing her special things and says she's coming to help me with mine. I think of their home with two children, a dog and cat and her own treasures to rescue. I tell her no, I'm fine. They will go North to stay with friends, out of danger. She wants me to come with them. I tell her I'll travel South—not crossing the city, not moving toward the fire. The heavier the smoke, the harder it is to breathe. This time, my car is full of gas. My hands are not trembling.

The phone rings and its Zev. "Come on over, you can stay all night here with us," he said, as I knew he would.

"But what if...?"

"Just come on over," I hear again, "We'll figure out what to do." The trouble is—their house might be in more danger than mine, and sure enough, soon after I arrive, they get a call that they have to evacuate. "I'll help you pack," I say, and just as we finish, another couple with their daughter, their son, and their dog, show up at the door.

Did Neal say—or did I say, "There's nothing we can do here. It will burn or it won't. Let's go to LA and have a party!" I think it was Neal who said that but I was thinking the same thing. We can't stop the flames but we can choose how to react to them. So off we go, three cars in tandem, two couples, two teenage girls and a boy, two dogs and me. I drive alone and unload my things at Mary's house in LA. She wants me to stay with her but I've already made a commitment. So it's on to the SLS hotel on La Cienega Blvd. The others have already arrived and checked us in. It is a festive place to say the least. Ultra modern. Decidedly playful.

We check the news on TV and the first thing I see is a beautiful house on Holly Road that is one of the first to burn. Tamara designed that beautiful home and was living there until two weeks ago when it was bought by a couple from LA. It's so hard to watch it covered in flames but I can't take my eyes off the screen. My daughter is gifted at restoring houses from the vision in her mind to the final detail and she was particularly attached to this one. I feel that history is repeating itself. At least the buyers didn't lose their personal treasures. At least they weren't living there. At least...I keep trying to find something else that turned out better than it might have.

At least no one died.

I keep watching. Will they show the mountain where my house is? It will be there when I return or it won't. No amount of worry will change the outcome. *Whatever happens I'll deal with it.* Suddenly, I realize that now when I say the words of that mantra, I believe them. It's no longer just my intention, it's finally just the way it is.

Zev calls my room and says it's time to go to dinner. Neal has worked magic, as usual, and we have a table at *Bazaar*, where it's impossible to get a reservation at the last minute, but here we are—all of us but the two dogs. Pooches' dinner will be served in their rooms.

We dine like this is our last meal and we will make the most of it. We tell stories and laugh hard at the smallest suggestion of humor. Everyone has their phones on vibrate. Every once in a while, someone has occasion to say, "There's absolutely nothing we can do. How about another glass of wine?" We don't even need a designated driver; we can walk from dinner to bed without crossing the street.

None of us would deny that this fire is a serious threat to our emotional and financial lives and to the city we love. We know the seriousness of the consequences. This wild foray is just our way of accepting life as it plays out. Our journey on earth is not predictable, no matter how much we wish it were.

The fire continues and we stay another night. We have breakfast on the rooftop of the hotel, tell more stories, get updates on the fire, walk the dogs, eat exotic food, call for more updates and finally check out of our most unusual safe-house.

I pick up my things at Mary's house and drive back to Santa Barbara. What a relief it is to see that I still have a home! No trees burned. No damage done. My friends on this grand excursion also come back to find their houses standing. As do Tamara and Jeff.

Others are not so fortunate. Two hundred and ten homes were destroyed in that fire. It is sobering news and at this moment, I'm feeling survivor's remorse. How could I have had such a wild celebration of life while so many people were living through the burning, going through the agony that once was mine?

But how would it have helped anyone if I had just imagined the worst, living in fear instead of gratitude?

Day passes, and then the night. The winds have softened and the ash lies thick upon cars and gardens, shrubs and bikes. The smoke lingers, as it will for days. I stay inside. I think about how different this experience is for me than the Tea House fire. And that strange celebration of life we created in LA—it wasn't denial. Someday I'll ask Zev if there's a psychological term for what that was. I would call it the acceptance of things I cannot change.

For All That Remains

Maybe by the time I reach the end of this life's journey, and angels lead me to the Light where my true loves wait, I'll know that it hasn't served me well to hold so tightly to possessions. I think how fragile this life is, how attachments to beautiful things bring such great pleasure but cause so much anxiety. It's what I cling to that binds me—it's what I release that sets me free.

It's now January 13, 2014. Al has been gone for six years. He always wanted me to make a good life for myself after he passed but the life I made wasn't what either of us expected.

Last year, or the year before, or the year before that—if I had met a man who intrigued me, who was making the world (or some part of the world) a better place, who was smart and witty and loved kids and dogs and books, who was passionate about life (and about me) I would probably no longer be widowed. But in all these years I never met a single man I would want to have a romantic dinner with, much less a breakfast. Certainly, not a dance. That could change, of course, though it's not likely.

But I am in love. In love with my children and their children and my friends and my dreams for the future. I'm in love with music and movies and telling stories and writing books and mentoring others. I'm in love with the people I work with who deal with grief, and chaos in all its forms. I'm in love with the shifting moods of the ocean and the gratitude I feel for having a capacity to notice the things that give me joy.

On my seventy-ninth birthday, I was lecturing in Berlin, invited by Hendrik Backarra and Professor Gerhard Huhn, who invited me there 25 years ago to speak in the *Kongresshalle*. The audience was smaller this time but no less enthusiastic. We created a fine seminar and I felt such joy in the doing of it. Twelve hours of teachings in four days on the subject, *Re-Inventing Your Future,* was a deeply satisfying experience. A woman who attended my seminar twenty-five years ago, brought me a thank you gift and a hug—after all this time! How sweet is that?

In June, two days after I turn eighty, I'll be teaching at the Santa Barbara Writers Conference. It is my great pleasure to be there. But now I hold the experience lightly in my hands, with delight but not attachment.

God isn't finished with me yet, so I want to be patient with myself regarding the lessons I'm still trying to learn. All those insights from my childhood and the stages of life that followed, remind me that I'm a risk-taker and stubborn besides. It's okay to make a fool of myself sometimes, to take an impossible challenge and fall short; the important thing is to accept and move on. I'm tenacious and vulnerable, a hard-working over-achiever, perhaps. I learned something from each of these remembered stories, some insights were more clarifying than others.

The message I learned from the fires, the losses, the stories and the tears is simply that love matters most of all and gratitude can tether you to life in the hardest times. There's a sense of empowerment in embracing the life that used to be, and honoring the hard times and the good times for they are both the building blocks that create the present and the future.

"What will I do now?" is a common question and it's natural to wonder. But the awareness that came to me is this: why not look at the future through a less focused lens and let it reveal options I might not have considered before? There are books to write and speeches to give, of course...but what else? New adventures may be waiting, just outside of my awareness. The choice is mine.

Whether I stay in Santa Barbara or live somewhere else, alone or with another, with a vibrant life or a quiet one, I know that this is the late afternoon of my life and *Whatever happens, I'll be fine—whatever comes, I'll deal with it.*

Tonight I embrace the unknown that tomorrow holds and whisper my gratitude for all that remains.

Photos:
As Time Goes By

I was 3, the year my dad shot the rattlesnake
just as I reached for it.

My senior year in high school, I was 16. No one would publish my novel or produce my screenplay. I decided it would be easier to be an actress. (What was I thinking?)

In my early 20's I had parts in six boring movies.
(Boring for the audience; fascinating for me.)

At 24, I retired to a more interesting life.
This is the photo Leonard kept on his desk.

When I was 38, my first book was published. Finally!
This was Al's favorite shot.

In four weeks, I'll be 80. Life is good.
I have more books to write,
more places to see, more hugs to give and receive.

In this story, I have omitted photos of Leonard (All the good ones burned) and of Al and the children, step-children and grandchildren because if I start, there's nowhere to stop. And later, great-grandchildren would regret not being included.

If you are dealing with loss, I hope these stories encourage you to look in your own rear view mirror and make a mental scrapbook of the memories that comfort you and strengthen you. Know that I wish you the best of all you can imagine.

Acknowledgments

It's taken eighty years for these stories to be lived, then processed, then adapted as a book. My loving parents and grandparents, thoughtful teachers and persistent hecklers all played their part, for I learned as much from my antagonists as from those who loved and nourished me. The wrinkles in my face have been hard-earned and I wear them with pride.

First-readers who critiqued my work in progress are Cleo Baldon, Mary Christianson, M.D., Zev Nathan, M.D., my daughters, Tamara Riley and Gina Somers, Pat Draghi, Marcia Orland and A. Paul Bergen. They made suggestions that added focus to the stories and Pam Headrick is the editor who corrected a plethora of spelling and punctuation errors, as did Madison Riley. The brilliant photographer, Jon Wimberely, offered me the use of one of his photographs for the jacket of the book. I've admired that picture for years. Jeff Rutherford, my son-in-law extraordinaire, was my finder of photos, fixer of computer problems and hero of all challenges.

My husbands, Leonard S. Picker and Albert N. Zdenek, MD, are greatly loved, and long passed. They shaped my life and I am grateful for them both. From Gina, came my first three grandchildren, Ashleigh, Taylor, and Cameron. The Riley girls number just two, Madison and McKenna. These are all at the heart of my happiness. Encouragement came from David V. Picker and Jean Picker Firstenberg, which means more to me than they probably realize.

About the Author

Marilee Zdenek is the best-selling author of six books and a pioneer in the application of brain research to enhance creativity.

The Right Brain Experience: An Intimate Program to Free the Powers of your Imagination was published in hardcover and paperback by McGraw Hill; it was re-published in paperback by Two Roads Publishing.

Marilee's other books include: *Inventing the Future: Advances in Imagery that Can Change Your Life, Someone Special,* and *Splinters in My Pride. God is a Verb!* and *Catch the New Wind* were written in collaboration with Marge Champion. *Someone Special* was adapted as a theatre piece and was performed at the Kennedy Center in Washington D.C. and The Dorothy Chandler Theater in Los Angeles.

Her pioneering work in the use of right-brain techniques for creativity and mental health led to a research project for Psychiatric Clinics of North America that was published in their medical journal. She presented programs for the White House Task Force on Innovative Learning, and gave five presentations at the The World Economic Forum in Davos, Switzerland. She has also spoken at the *Kongresshalle* in Berlin, Stanford University, University of Southern California, and University of California Santa Barbara. For twenty-five years, she taught at the Santa Barbara Writers Conference. Marilee served as Vice President and Literary Awards Chairperson for Pen West (now PEN CENTER, USA).

As Founder/President of Right-Brian Resources, Inc., Marilee has lectured for many corporations in the United

States and Europe. Her work has been recognized by Barbara Walters, *Newsweek*, *The Today Show*, *Los Angeles Times*, *The Washington Post*, and many others in the U.S. and Europe. Currently, Marilee is on the Board of Directors of Hospice of Santa Barbara, where she leads programs for medical professionals on how to use guided imagery to comfort patients who are at the end of their lives and to give emotional support to their families.

Marilee's website is helpful for readers who want to know more about her work:
www.MarileeZdenek.com

She always likes to hear from her readers. Her email address is:
Marilee@MarileeZdenek.com

And the Critics Said....

"At least once a month, I take one of Marilee Zdenek's books off the shelf and read some of the things she's written because I think they are so wonderful."
– CHARLES SCHULZ, Creator of "PEANUTS"

"THE RIGHT-BRAIN EXPERIENCE is a warm, well-written and even inspiring self-help book."
– Los Angeles Times

"Marilee Zdenek provides a practical structure for making dreams come true."
– BETTY EDWARDS, Drawing on the Right Side of the Brain

"Marilee Zdenek is one of our most popular speakers—it is always a pleasure to have her with us."
– KLAUS SCHWAB, President WORLD ECONOMIC FORUM, Davos, Switzerland

"She is a master at presenting her material; the audience was completely captivated."
– GERHARDT HUHN, Bewusst Sein, Berlin Kulturstadt, Berlin, Germany

"I am impressed with the presentation by Marilee Zdenek. Her material is intriguing and quite powerful."
– GUNNAR WESSMAN, President, Pharmecia AB, Upsala, Sweden

"The highly professional quality of her work was evident and the material she presented was compelling. Our understanding of imagery and imagination was enhanced as a result of the experiences she guided us through and the insights she offered."
– PAUL R. MESSIER, Director, White House Task Force on Innovative Learning

"I have experienced many presentations and workshops directed toward evoking right-brain experience and rank Marilee Zdenek's at the very top."
– ROBERT McKIM, Professor of Engineering, Stanford University

"THE RIGHT-BRAIN EXPERIENCE facilitates the reader's ability to experience life as a journey of infinite self-discovery and creative expression."
– KLAUS D. HOPPE, MD, PhD., Associate Professor of Clinical Psychiatry, UCLA

"Hurrah! And I say congratulations to you, Marilee Zdenek. You make people aware of what we have been given to use."
– STEVIE WONDER, Composer, Singer, Musician

"Marilee Zdenek shows us how to expand our own brain power to find faster and better ways to solve difficult problems—easily!"
– SPENCER JOHNSON, M.D., Co-Author of *The One Minute Manager*

"I highly recommend this program to all people who are interested in developing their imaginations and gaining control of their lives."
– BRUCE CHRISTIANSON, M.D., Psychiatrist

"I know from my own experience that Marilee Zdenek's techniques of right-brain imaging are remarkably successful in stimulating memory and creativity, but also in helping to cope with strong emotions. She has done a great service in making (this program) available."
– CHARLES CHAMPLIN, *Los Angeles Times*, Arts Critic Emeritus

"Marilee is a storyteller, but she is more than that. She is an understanding presence that can make immeasurable differences in our ability to bounce back after the stress of events we cannot control...the sound of her voice, as gentle and soothing as

honey…Coming to us when our personal pack of trouble is weighing us down, through reality and imagination, she helps us to feel safe again."
– JEAN SPENCER, *Ventura County Star*

"INVENTING THE FUTURE *leads us to realize that we have greater power of choice in our lives than most of us dared to imaging.*
– GABRIELE L. RICO, Ph.D. *Writing the Natural Way*

"Tell me what you imagine and I will tell you who you are. Let me tell you what to imagine and I will tell you what, gradually, you will become.
INVENTING THE FUTURE *is a book with a great deal to give to those able to receive it."*
– JACK MILES, Pulitzer Prize Winner, *God: A Biography*

"An unforgettable experience—magical, practical and life-changing."
– RON FIELD, award winning Broadway choreographer.

Made in the USA
Charleston, SC
07 June 2014